STO

MARK TWAIN
Novelist, Humorist, Satirist,
Grassroots Historian and
America's Unpaid Goodwill Ambassador at Large
ROBIN McKOWN

Mark Twain

MARK TWAIN

Novelist, Humorist, Satirist,
Grassroots Historian and
America's Unpaid Goodwill Ambassador at Large

ROBIN McKOWN

McGraw-Hill Book Company
New York • St. Louis • San Francisco
Montreal • Toronto

For Aimé and Saholy Rakotodrainibe

Library of Congress Cataloging in Publication Data

McKown, Robin.
  Mark Twain.

  SUMMARY: A biography stressing the wide range of
literary achievements of the author considered by many
to be America's greatest writer.
  1. Clemens, Samuel Langhorne, 1835–1910—Biography—
Juvenile literature. [1. Clemens, Samuel Langhorne,
1835–1910. 2. Authors, American] I. Title.
PS1331.M24   818'.4'03 [B] [92]   74-9583
ISBN 0-07-045368 (lib. bdg.)

123456789 MUBP 78987654

other books by robin mckown

Nonfiction
The Congo, River of Mystery
The American Revolution: The French Allies
The Image of Puerto Rico
Heroic Nurses
The Story of the Incas
Thomas Paine
Marie Curie
The Fabulous Isotopes
Giant of the Atom: Ernest Rutherford
She Lived for Science: Irène Joliot-Curie
Seven Famous Trials
Colonial Conquest of Africa
Republic of the Zaïre
Maximilian
Opium War in China
Lumumba
Nkrumah
Crisis in South Africa
The World of Mary Cassatt

Fiction
The Boy Who Woke up in Madagascar
Girl of Madagascar
Rakoto and the Drongo Bird
Janine
Patriot of the Underground

table of contents

1

a boy named sam clemens

My mother had a good deal of trouble with me but I
think she enjoyed it.

—Mark Twain

At the age of two weeks, Mark Twain overheard his
family discussing various names for him. Abraham,
Isaac, and Jacob were praised but rejected. Then his
father said, "Samuel is a very excellent name."

Whereupon the baby laid down his rattle and
announced in a loud firm voice: "Father I cannot,

cannot wear the name of Samuel . . . Father, I have an invincible antipathy to that name."

No one paid him any heed. He was duly christened Samuel Langhorne Clemens. There was nothing he could do about it—at the time.

He told this story about himself many years later. There is no reason to suspect it of being less truthful than any of his other tall tales—such as the one about the talking blue jay who kept dropping nuts down the chimney of a miner's shack, thinking he was hoarding them for the winter.

Sam Clemens' birthplace was a two-room cabin in Florida, Missouri, a backwoods hamlet of about a hundred population. On the date of his birth, November 30, 1835, Halley's Comet had traveled its orbit to the point nearest the sun and was receding.

The Clemens of Virginia traced their ancestors back to seventeenth-century England. According to family legend, one Geoffrey Clement, a judge, helped sentence King Charles I to death. From that time on they had had an off-and-on connection with the legal profession. Sam's father, John Marshall Clemens, acquired a document entitling him to practice law from a Kentucky lawyer to whom he was briefly apprenticed.

In 1823, he married Sam's mother, a beautiful Kentucky belle, Jane Lampton. They moved to Tennessee, where Clemens became a small-town postmaster, and where he was able, in a moment of relative prosperity, to invest several hundred dollars in a vast tract of land, at least 75,000 acres. This was to be a legacy for his children. The only one who would profit from it was the future Mark Twain; he did so by writing a novel and a play about the legacy.

John Clemens took his family to Florida, Missouri, to join his wife's brother-in-law, John Quarles, in running a country store. Clemens had no talents for storekeeping. In 1839, when Sam was four, they moved on to Hannibal, Missouri.

Hannibal was a drowsy sun-drenched town on the banks of the Mississippi, surrounded by woodlands. It was an ideal spot for a young boy to grow up in. It was exactly like St. Petersburg, the setting of Mark Twain's *The Adventures of Tom Sawyer*.

Sam was the Clemens' sixth child, but three of the older ones died young or in infancy. There remained Orion, ten years older than Sam, and black-haired Pamela, who was eight years Sam's senior. He had a younger brother, Henry, whom—he later stressed— was not a bit like Tom Sawyer's young tattletale brother, Sid. Their household also included a slave girl, Jennie.

Sam had no idea that slavery was wrong. The church claimed that slavery was the "will of God." The town notables approved it; for them the most serious crime was to help a slave escape. The Clemens acquired a little slave boy named Sandy. He was always singing. Mrs. Clemens told Sam she liked to hear him sing; it showed he was not thinking about the family he would never see again. Once Sam saw some slaves, roped together, waiting miserably on the dock to be transported down river. "Down river" they would be put at hard labor on the plantations; most of them would die of brutal treatment within a few years' time. The man who bought slaves to sell down river was known as a "nigger trader" and generally despised.

When the Clemens arrived in Hannibal, Sam's father bought some property in the center of town, built a white frame house on Hill Street for the family, and set up a law office in a clapboard building. His clients were few but the town made him a Justice of the Peace, which provided a meager living and carried with it the formidable title of *Judge*. He was a gaunt, spare unsmiling man, who stalked the house like a scourge of God.

In contrast, Mrs. Clemens was witty and fun-loving and so kindhearted she prayed for the Devil —since no one else would. She petted her children, scolded them, forgave them their sins, doused them with all manner of patent medicines, convinced each time they would work miracles. She cared little for housework but did lovely embroidery.

In this atmosphere of hot and cold, Sam Clemens grew from a sickly infant to an undersized husky boy with red curly hair, blue-gray eyes, a southern drawl like his mother's, and a roguish humor. When he was seven an older girl taunted him for not smoking. A year later he was smoking cheap cigars. He grumbled about school, and of an obnoxious teacher named William Cross, he wrote:

> Cross by name and cross by nature,
> Cross jumped over an Irish potato.

Nor did he have any affection for Sunday School. According to his reminiscences, he plagued his teacher, Mr. Barclay, about Eve, asking why she did not run away when she saw the serpent in the apple tree, as most women would. Barclay refused to answer and rebuked him for meddling in matters beyond his comprehension.

The pranks and adventures in which Sam Clemens was involved were identical, or similar, to those of the fictional Tom Sawyer. Sam was in love with a little girl with blond pigtails named Laura Hawkins. Tom's sweetheart was Becky Thatcher. Sam and Laura were lost in the maze of McDowell's Cave, a mile and a half south of Hannibal. Tom and Becky had their ordeal in McDougal's Cave.

Near the Clemens home was a dilapidated barn of a house where Tom Blankenship lived with his drunken father and seven ragged brothers and sisters. Tom Blankenship did not have to go to school or church, or dress in good clothes, and could hunt and fish in the woods any time he wished. Sam regarded him with the same envy that Tom Sawyer regarded his friend, Huck Finn. Bence Blankenship,

Tom's older brother, once secretly fed a runaway slave for a week, setting a precedent for Huck Finn's championship of "Nigger Jim."

A democratic spirit pervaded Hannibal. People had a poor opinion of anyone who put on airs, like young Neil Moss, son of a rich pork packer, who came back from Yale in "swell eastern clothes." Mark Twain would turn him into Tom Driscoll in *The Tragedy of Pudd'nhead Wilson.* Hannibal had its quota of respectable church-going folk, but it had a seamier side too. Gangs of rowdies rode the streets shooting up the town, as in a western movie. Men were shot down on whims. Tom Sawyer saw one murder. Sam witnessed three or four.

A gentle farmer named Smarr became impudent when he drank. Sam was ten when he saw Smarr killed for something he said. During the next couple of years he witnessed a man kill his slave with a chunk of slag, the stabbing to death of a young Californian with a bowie knife, some boys forcing their harmless old uncle onto his knees; the old man was saved only because the revolver one of them held to his head did not go off.

From his seventh to his twelfth year, Sam spent part of every summer on the 500-acre farm of his jovial Uncle John Quarles, who had prospered as his father had not. Even in old age, Mark Twain remembered "the faint odors of the wildflowers . . . the far-off hammering of woodpeckers . . . the snapshot glimpses of disturbed wild creatures scurrying

14

through the grass," and everything else about those wonderful summers. Especially the table laden with fried chicken, roast pig, wild turkey, venison, pheasants, rabbits, hot corn pone. "The North thinks it knows how to make corn bread," he would say scornfully, "but this is a gross superstition."

Uncle John's 20-some slaves lived down the road in their own quarters and always seemed glad to see the children of their white master. In one cabin was an ancient bedridden woman, who, the children were told, was more than 1000 years old and had once talked to Moses. Sam's favorite was Uncle Dan'l, who was a gold mine of fascinating stories, including "The Golden Arm," which Mark Twain would tell over and over to amuse and scare his lecture audiences. It had to do with a stingy man who buried his wife, and then, remembering that she had a golden arm, went to dig it up and take it home with him.

Judge Clemens' affairs went from bad to worse. Debts forced him to move his family from Hill Street to rooms over a local drugstore. One night he was caught on the highway in a storm and came down with pneumonia. Sam was not yet twelve when his father died. His gentle handsome brother Orion went to St. Louis to work as a printer to help support the family. After school Sam did odd jobs, clerked in a grocery store, delivered papers, whatever he could get.

Sometime in 1848, he quit school and became an

apprentice to Joseph Ament, owner of the Hannibal *Gazette*. As an apprentice, he had to build the morning fire, fetch water from the pump, sweep, sort type, set type, wet down paper stock, wash rollers and frames, wrap 350 papers for mailing, deliver 100 more by hand each week. A young journeyman who was there remembered Sam Clemens as a little sandy-haired boy, seated on a high box at the type case, smoking a big cigar as he worked. He slept on a pallet on the printing house floor and ate cabbage stew at the Ament table.

Sam was still with Ament in 1849 when a cholera epidemic caused some 30 deaths and a yellow fever epidemic claimed even more victims. His mother dosed him with a patent medicine called "Pain Killer" and he stayed well. In 1850, when news of the California Gold Rush reached Hannibal, about .60 citizens, smitten with gold fever, left for the west. Sam was too young to catch that malady.

That summer Orion returned from St. Louis and started a rival weekly newspaper, the *Western Union*, buying a press and type from his savings. In January, 1851, he hired Sam from the *Gazette* at $3.50 a week, a princely salary which Orion was never prosperous enough to pay. During his first month working for his brother, Sam broke into print with a short piece about a fire that had broken out next door to the printing office. He ended with the irrefutable comment of a fellow apprentice, Jim Wolfe: "If that thar fire hadn't bin put out, there'd a bin the greatest *confirmation* of the age!" His role as a humorist was established.

His sister Pamela married Will Moffett that year, and went to St. Louis to live. Orion borrowed $500 from a farmer and took over the Hannibal *Journal*. To please subscribers, he ran their children's school compositions; he carried almost no local news. In September, 1852, Orion went off on a trip and left Sam in charge. He had a marvelous time that month printing jokes and stories about family brawls. It became obvious that without Sam, Orion's paper would have been a dull and deadly publication.

Sam wrote a sketch called "The Dandy Frightening the Squatter," during this period, sent it to the *Carpet Bag* in Boston, signed SLC, and forgot it. Twenty years after his death, a researcher discovered that the story had been printed.

When Sam was eighteen, a drunken tramp stopped him and asked for a light for his pipe. Later that night the drunk was thrown into the one-cell calaboose for causing trouble in the Negro section of town. The drunk's straw mattress caught fire; Sam was convinced that his matches had caused it. The sheriff, who had the only key, could not be reached. Sam was there with others to break down the door with a battering ram but they were too late. For years Sam was haunted by the memory of the tramp's face behind the window bars, framed by the roaring flames.

Those eighteen years, fourteen of them spent in

Hannibal, were the most crucial of his life. Tragedy and comedy, hypocrites and outlaws, good people and bad, all added up to a boyhood rich in human interest and drama. Sam Clemens absorbed it all, the folklore of the women and slaves, the superstitions of the men, the stories he heard, the flavor and rhythm of people's speech. Again and again he would call on this raw material for his books and sketches.

In 1853, he decided to go see the World's Fair in New York. He boarded a steamboat for St. Louis and worked for the *Evening News* long enough to earn his fare east. When he reached New York City he had three dollars in change and a ten dollar bill sewed in the lining of his coat. At the fair, he saw the new crystal palace and a safety elevator invented by a Vermont mechanic named Elisha Otis, among other wonders. To pay for his room and board, he took a job with a New York printer "at villainous wages."

In those days a journeyman printer could find work anywhere. Tired of New York after a while, he went to Philadelphia where he worked for three different newspapers. He had gone on to Washington, D.C. when Orion wrote him that he had given up the Hannibal *Journal* and moved to Muscatine, Iowa, with their mother and young Henry. He wanted Sam to come help him run the Muscatine *Journal*. Sam went to his aid. A few months later he was helping Orion run another newspaper in Keokuk,

Iowa, where Orion had married a girl named Mollie. It was all wasted time, so far as Sam was concerned. He saw clearly that Orion did not have the makings of a newspaperman.

An account of the explorations in the Amazon Valley of a certain Lieutenant Herndon caught his fancy. From what Herndon said, he judged one could make a fortune by starting a cocoa plantation. He decided to have a try at it. In 1856 he worked in a printing office in Cincinnati for five months to earn enough money for the trip. Then he booked passage down the Mississippi on an ancient vessel called the *Paul Jones* to New Orleans, certain he could get a ship there to take him to Brazil. He was twenty-one that year. He felt himself a man and had a fair share of confidence in his abilities.

2

mississippi pilot

Your true pilot cares nothing about anything on earth
but the river, and his pride in his occupation surpasses
the pride of kings.

—Mark Twain

The mate of the *Paul Jones* had a red woman and a
blue woman tattooed on his right arm, and a blue
anchor tied with a red rope between them. Once
Sam Clemens heard him roaring for someone to
bring him a capstan bar. Sam timidly offered to go
get it. The mate's look of amazed contempt might

have been that of the Emperor of Russia to a rag-picker who had offered to carry out a diplomatic mission.

Like all Hannibal boys, Sam had always been fascinated by steamboat life. Now for the first time he felt part of the ship family. Snubbed by the tattooed mate, he made friends with the night watchman, who told him a series of increasingly incredible adventures. Discovery that the watchman was a humbug and a liar of the first order broke the spell. But before the trip was over he was on good terms with one of the pilots, Horace E. Bixby, who let him do some steering on the daylight watches.

Pilots were the elite of the river men. Not even the captain could give them orders. Their salaries were high. Off duty, they wore polished silk hats, fancy shirts, diamond breastpins, kid gloves, patent leather boots. Pilots were great talkers; their talk was always about the river. Bixby was one of the top men in this profession; some ranked him as the best pilot the river had ever known.

In New Orleans, Sam was told that no ships were scheduled for Brazil and that it was unlikely there would be any for the next century. Having no friends in New Orleans and little money, Sam went back to the ship and asked Bixby if he would train him to be a Mississippi River pilot. Bixby was not enthusiastic, but Sam kept pestering him until he agreed. Bixby would teach Sam what he knew for $500; $100 to be paid in advance, the rest from his future wages. Pestered further, he consented to wait for the $100 until they reached St. Louis and Sam could borrow it from his brother-in-law, Pamela's husband, William Moffett.

When they were pulling out of New Orleans, Bixby gave him the wheel and told him to "shave those steamships as close as you'd peel an apple." In half a minute, Sam had a wide margin between the *Paul Jones* and the other vessels. Bixby flayed him with abuse, seized the wheel, and trimmed them so closely collision seemed inevitable. When he had calmed down, he explained to his apprentice that one must hug the bank going upstream to take advantage of the easy water beyond the current. Until then, Sam had the illusion that all a pilot need do was to keep his vessel in the water—and he saw that that would not be difficult since the river was so wide.

As they proceeded Bixby called his attention to Six Mile Point, Nine Mile Point, Twelve Mile Point. Sam thought he was making conversation. Later on Bixby ordered him to name the first point above New Orleans. He admitted that he could not name any location they had passed. Bixby wrathfully informed him he did not have enough sense to pilot a cow down a lane. Then he said gently that Sam must get a notebook and write down everything he told him; to be a pilot one must learn the entire river.

By the time they reached St. Louis, Sam's notebook "bristled" with names of towns, points, bars, islands, bends. It still was on paper, not in his head. Moreover, it represented only half of the journey; the four alternate hours when he and Bixby had been on watch.

At St. Louis, Bixby, with Sam, quit the ancient *Paul Jones* for an imposing New Orleans steamer, which had a long gilded saloon and an oil painting "by some gifted sign painter" on every stateroom door. The pilot house was a glass temple with a sofa and red and gold window curtains. Black waiters with white aprons brought them tarts and ices and coffee at midwatch. Nonetheless Sam was depressed. He had found out that all he had learned coming up river would be useless on the return journey. He would have to commence from scratch.

Nor was it enough to learn towns, bends, and islands. He had to know every old snag or drowned cottonwood along the 1,200 mile bank. He must be able to pass within arm's reach of a sunken and invisible wreck that might easily destroy the steamer in five minutes. Every time Sam thought he was making progress, Bixby floored him with something new.

What is the shape of Walnut Bend? Respectfully, Sam told him that he did not know it had a shape. Bixby exploded again. One must know the *shape* of the river to be able to steer at night. Starlight threw certain shadows which gave the river a different shape than it had on a pitch dark night. Mist and moonlight altered the scene in other ways. In despair, Sam asked if he had to memorize the shape of the river under all these forms. Bixby reassured him that he had only to memorize the river's *actual* shape and keep that one in mind.

Nor did the river always retain the same shape. Banks caved in, altering the shoreline. Over the years the river moved sidewise, to the right or the left. Thinking of all this, Sam figured out that in this his chosen profession he must first learn more than any man ought to be allowed to know and learn it all over again in twenty-four hours.

During the last period of his apprenticeship, Bixby loaned him to a Mr. Brown, pilot of the *Pennsylvania*. In contrast to Bixby, whom Sam admired and respected, Brown was a devil to work for. According to Brown, everything Sam did or thought of doing was wrong. If he could not find a pretext to find fault, he invented one. Sam passed his off-duty hours in conjuring all sorts of fantastic ways to murder his chief.

Sam's younger brother Henry also had a job on the *Pennsylvania*, as a mud clerk. Mud clerks received no pay but could be promoted to the paying posts of third clerk, second clerk, on up to purser. There came a day when Brown turned his evil temper on Henry. Henry had delivered a message to him from the captain, but Brown, being deaf, had not heard it. He accused Henry of not giving the message. When Henry insisted he had done so, Brown yelled for him to get out and started after him down the ladder with a ten-pound lump of coal in his hand.

Sam's long, pent-up wrath erupted. He knocked Brown down with a heavy stool, then pounded him with his fists until the pilot wrested himself free and sprang for the neglected wheel.

Captain John Klinefelter called Sam to task, lectured him about the seriousness of his offense, said he must never do such a thing on his ship again, then confessed that he was "deuced glad" it had happened and hinted it would not be a bad idea for someone to give Brown a good thrashing when he was ashore.

Brown also went to the captain and said he would not stay on the same boat with the "cub." Klinefelter actually offered Sam his job, but Sam did not yet feel himself a full-fledged pilot, and left the steamer in New Orleans. Henry stayed on.

Four days later Sam heard that the *Pennsylvania* had blown up sixty miles below Memphis and that 150 men had lost their lives. The pilot Brown disappeared and was never heard of again. The captain, who was in the barber's chair at the time, was not hurt nor was the barber. Henry was less fortunate. Sam found him at the Memphis hospital in a room with 30 or 40 other men suffering from wounds or burns. He died six days later, possibly through an overdose of morphine given by an inexperienced medical student. In some obscure way it seemed to Sam that he was to blame for the catastrophe, if only because he saw so clearly that his quarrel with Brown had saved his own life.

On April 9, 1859, a Pilot's Certificate was granted to Samuel L. Clemens by the District of St. Louis inspectors. It stated that he was "a suitable and safe person to be entrusted with the powers and duties of Pilot of Steam·Boats." At last he was on his own.

In the next three years he piloted ships ranging from old tugs to *The City of Memphis*, the largest on the river with the reputation of being the hardest to pilot. He earned $250 a month, more than his father had ever earned. Off watch, he talked with passengers, watched men play poker in saloon games, sometimes saw pistols flash and gamblers fall. He played the piano, sang river songs, danced with the ladies, and became as expert as anyone at telling river tales.

He wore sideburns, but no mustache as yet. When he was off-duty he stayed with Pamela and Will Moffett in St. Louis and wore patent leather shoes, bow ties, a starched shirt front—all the fancy clothes that were the insignia of the Mississippi river pilot.

Passengers, officers, and crew provided him with a new supply of human material to add to his Hannibal reservoir. He later claimed that whenever he found a well-drawn character in fiction or biography, he took a warm personal interest for the reason that he had "met him on the river."

He had little time for writing but he did one piece for a New Orleans paper, a lampoon on the rather pedantic articles written by a retired pilot named Captain Isaiah Sellers. He once said that Sellers signed his articles "Mark Twain" and that he, Sam Clemens, stole his pseudonym. He was maligning himself. Sellers never signed himself "Mark Twain," a riverboat cry meaning that the water was two fathoms (or 12 feet) deep, and thus safe for the ship to pass.

Sam Clemens, soon to be better known as Mark Twain, was in New Orleans on January 26, 1861, when word came through that Louisiana had opted to leave the Union. His ship headed north the next day. The last night of their voyage, batteries at Jefferson Barracks below St. Louis fired two shots through the steamer chimneys.

Regular river runs ceased when the Civil War broke out on April 12, 1861. Mark Twain's glorious days as a Mississippi pilot were brought to an abrupt close. For years the well-being, even the existence, of the Mississippi Valley population had depended on steamboat traffic. It would never be the same again. By the time the war was over, railroads would be replacing steamboats. Pilots would be losing their glamour. A romantic era would have ended.

3

non-hero of the civil war

I could have become a soldier myself if I had waited.
I had got part of it learned, I knew more about retreating
than the man that invented retreating.

—Mark Twain

The beginning of the Civil War led to considerable
confusion in the middle west and border states. Many
people could not decide which side they were on.
Mark Twain was one of those caught in the middle.
In the 1860 election, he had sided with the moderates
who wanted peace and the preservation of the

Union. He subsequently wrote several articles for the New Orleans *Daily Crescent,* signed "Snodgrass," in which he ridiculed army life. Though born in a slave state and the son of a slaveholder, he recognized the evils of slavery and at the time of the outbreak of hostilities, his sympathies were with the North. The Rebel group in Missouri was very active and noisy, but their opponents were more powerful; Missouri voted to remain in the Union. That did not end the conflict among fellow Missourians. Mark Twain returned to Hannibal for a spell early in June 1861 and was swamped with anti-Union talk. Union forces were entering Missouri. The pro-Southern governer, Claiborne Fox Jackson, issued a proclamation calling for 50,000 militia to repel them. Mark Twain was one of 15 young men of Hannibal who responded to this appeal. It seemed, for the moment, the patriotic thing to do. They met in secret and formed their own company. They called themselves the Marion Rangers, since Hannibal was in Marion County.

None had military experience but that did not trouble them. As their captain they chose an energetic young man named Tom Lyman. Mark Twain was made second lieutenant. They never did have a first lieutenant. Orderly sergeant was Jo Bowers, "a huge, good-natured, flax-headed lubber . . . a grumbler by nature . . . and often a quite picturesque liar." Handsome, graceful, "neat-as-a-cat" Ed Stevens became a corporal. In his own account, *The Private*

History of a Campaign That Failed, published years later, Mark Twain said the boys did not know whether sergeant or corporal ranked higher, so Stevens and Bowers were granted equal rank. He likely exaggerated.

So far as most of them were concerned, they considered this military adventure as a holiday. A few of them would later become disciplined soldiers. Smith, the blacksmith apprentice, a "fast donkey" with a "slow and sluggish nature, but a soft heart," would lose his life in battle. That any one of them could be killed was not conceivable at the time.

Their first maneuver was a march to New London, Missouri, ten miles distant. Carrying their old rifles or shotguns, they set out one dark night. The first hour was filled with nonsense and laughing, but the merriment oozed out of them during the gloomy march and talk dried up. In about two hours they neared a log farmhouse where it was said five Union soldiers were staying.

Captain Lyman called a halt and in a whisper proposed a plan of attack. It occurred to them for the first time they were facing actual war. In their response "there was no hesitation, no indecision," Mark Twain would write. They said that Lyman could meddle with those Union soldiers if he wished, but he would have to wait a long time if he expected them to follow him. As an alternative, they would "flank the farm-house," that is, go around it—which they did. They felt very cheerful afterward at the success of their first military strategy.

Near dawn they straggled into New London, suffering only blisters on their heels. Colonel Rall, a Rebel sympathizer who had fought in the Mexican War, gave them breakfast and a speech "full of glory and gunpowder," in which he urged them to swear on the Bible to be faithful to the State of Missouri and drive all invaders from her soil—no matter whose flag the invaders carried. It was all very inspiring but confusing.

Later in the morning they formed a line of battle, "pierced the forest" about half a mile, and took up a strong position by a creek—where part of the command went swimming and the others fished. After that they occupied an old maple sugar camp near the farm of a sympathetic farmer named Mason. Neighbors of his brought them mules and horses as a loan for the length of the war, which they figured would last about three months. These town soldiers were unable even to stay on their mounts at first.

Mark Twain, as second lieutenant, ordered Sergeant Bowers to feed his mule. Bowers said the lieutenant had better get out of his head any notion that he had gone to war to be dry nurse to a mule. Mark felt this was insubordination but let it pass.

No one wanted the degrading title of camp cook so they had no dinner. They spent the afternoon dozing under trees, smoking their pipes, and talking about their sweethearts; by supper time they were famished. Their dilemma was solved by everyone pitching in to gather wood, build fires, and prepare their food. They went to bed in a long corncrib, leaving a horse tied to the door as a guard. Trustfully they felt he would neigh should a stranger approach.

For a few days life was "idly delicious, it was perfect." Then their farmer friends reported a rumor that the enemy was advancing toward them. Lyman, their captain, again urged them to take a stand, but he was overruled by a vote of the majority, including privates. The vote was for retreat which they began that night. To make better time, they left their horses and donkeys behind. In the dark, they lost their footing on a slippery hill and fell one on top of the other, ending in the brook at the bottom. In the muddle they lost much of their ammunition. Sometime after nine they were back at Farmer Mason's farm. He commented that they were a curious breed of soldiers, and that he guessed the war would end quickly because no government could stand the expense of the shoe leather they used up retreating.

About two that morning a horseman woke up the household, shouting that a detachment of Union soldiers were on their way with orders to hang any bands like theirs they could find. No one doubted his story. The boys spent the rest of the night, wretchedly, in a ravine, drowned by rain, deafened by a howling wind and thunder. Near dawn a black servant came and said the alarm was false and that they could all come back to breakfast.

They spent several rather boring days at the Mason farm, going to bed at sunset as their hosts did, and were almost happy with the next rumor that the enemy was on their track. This time they retreated all the way to Camp Ralls—their first post.

That night they decided they should have a picket in army fashion. Mark ordered Sergeant Bowers to stand guard. Bowers refused. The other men refused too, some because of the weather, the rest saying frankly they would not go out in any kind of weather. Their refusal to obey orders was in the best spirit of independent Americans, but it complicated things. Eventually Mark coaxed Bowers into picket duty by offering to exchange ranks with him and go along as his subordinate. They stood out in the rain for a couple of hours, then they went back to bed. That was the only time the Marion Rangers tried to establish a night watch.

Rumors of enemies hovering near grew so frequent that they finally said let them hover; the Rangers stayed put. One night when they were barracked in a log cabin, a lone horseman rode up. Certain he was the long expected enemy, they aimed their guns at him through the chinks between the logs. Someone panicked and shouted "fire!" They pulled their triggers. The man fell from his horse and was dead when they went out to examine him. He wore no

uniform, carried no arms, and might have been anybody. Nor did his reinforcements appear.

That was the night Mark Twain decided he had
no stomach for war and killing. Yet he stayed on a
little longer to engage in a few more strategic re-
treats. In a camp in Florida, the town where Sam
Clemens was born, the men heard that a Union
colonel with an entire regiment was sweeping down
on them. For once the story was true. Mark Twain
and about half of their outfit rode off for good.

On their way they met Brigadier General Thomas
Harris, who held the title of commander of all the
militia in the region. Before the war Tom Harris had
been the Hannibal telegraph operator. They liked
him but could not take him seriously as a general.
When he ordered them back to duty, they informed
him it looked like there would be a little disturbance
so they had concluded to go home.

Mark Twain learned later that the Union colonel
he had not felt inclined to meet was Ulysses S.
Grant, then almost as unknown as he was. In future
writings he would turn his gifts of sarcasm and irony
on pompous military commanders; for Grant he always retained respect and admiration. As for himself, he had seen enough of the folly and madness
of war to last a lifetime.

Nor did he ever feel any shame afterward in talking about the nonheroic adventures of the Marion
Rangers. On at least one occasion he did so before
a veterans' reunion—and had them all rolling in their
seats with laughter.

4

secretary to the secretary of nevada territory

If you are of any account, stay at home and make your way by faithful diligence; but if you are 'no account,' go away from home, and then you will *have* to work, whether you want to or not.

CO. SCHOOLS —Mark Twain
C821321

Mark's brother, Orion, whom he had been supporting from his pilot's salary, had a stroke of good luck. Edward Bates, a friend from Orion's St. Louis days, was appointed to President Lincoln's Cabinet. He got Orion the post of Secretary to the Governor in

35

the Territory of Nevada. Since Orion still needed help to get to Nevada, he signed Mark on as his secretary. Mark paid $300 for fare for both of them on the twenty-day stagecoach trip to Carson City, the capital.

On July 25, 1861, shortly after Mark's resignation from the militia, they set out in a great stagecoach drawn by "six handsome steeds." The weather was superb; the landscape "brilliant with sunshine." Abandoning his fancy clothes, Mark wore a rough, heavy suit, a woolen army shirt, and boots. In Orion's baggage were about four pounds of United States government statutes and a six-pound unabridged dictionary. They had several blankets, pipes, five pounds of tobacco, and, as protection from Indians, a Smith & Wesson seven shooter and a Colt revolver.

Nearly every day they took a new driver. All of them told lurid tales. One man claimed the Apaches used to keep him "so leaky with bullet-holes" that he "couldn't hold his vittles," and came near to starving.

The "vittles" at the stage stations were the least pleasant part of their journey. They were served bacon condemned by the United States Army, and a beverage called "slumgullion," which pretended to be tea but tasted like a concoction of dishrag, sand, and stale bacon rind.

At one station they met a friendly, soft-spoken official named Jack Slade, who courteously insisted on pouring Mark Twain the last coffee in the pot. In

his book about his western experiences, *Roughing It,*
Mark Twain would say he was trembling in his
boots lest his host regret his generosity and draw
his gun. The truth was he did not learn until later
that Slade was the notorious gunman, already reputed to have shot down twenty-six men.

Carson City, which they reached on August 14,
was a spot of desert in a cloud of alkali dust, walled
in by barren mountains. Its main street had rows of
white frame stores packed together. Its plaza was an
unfenced vacant lot useful for auctions, horse trad-
ing, or town meetings. Population was then around
2,000.

Governor of Nevada Territory, James W. Nye,
a former police commissioner of New York City,
lived in style in a one-story, two-room house. A handsome, courtly, white-haired man, he was said to have
shaken hands with everyone in the territory before
he had held office a year. He had gained even more
respect in this rough frontier country by his ability
to drink anyone under the table.

The rest of the government officials lived in boarding houses, their bedrooms serving as offices. Orion
and Mark shared a room in the home of Bridget
O'Flannigan, which they furnished with a bed, a
small table, two chairs, a government fireproof safe,
and their unabridged dictionary. Board and room
cost them ten dollars.

Orion earned $1,800 a year which would have gone
a long way except that he was so scrupulously hon-

est he usually ended up paying for all the small items classified as government disbursements. During Nye's frequent trips out of town, Orion took over his work and was rewarded by being called "Governor" himself. This pleased Mollie when she came to join him.

Mark Twain had no salary, but then he had nothing to do either. To pass the time, he hiked to Lake Tahoe with a friend named Johnny. The sheet of blue water walled in by snowclad peaks seemed to Mark "the fairest picture the whole earth affords." On the lake shore they found a cache of food in an earlier camp and helped themselves. The next day they took a boat they found up shore, claimed 300 acres as their own, and built a brush house to enforce that claim.

They spent three weeks in this wilderness, then left to borrow more provisions from the cache. On their return they found a forest fire raging—the result of a cook fire not properly extinguished. No guilt feelings of a later ecology-conscious generation marred Mark's awe at the sublime spectable of great crimson spirals repeated in the lake's mirror. Only when it was over were the youths struck with the realization they had lost everything. Abandoning their claim, they went back to Carson City, hungry and empty-handed.

All manner of stories were floating around town about the fortunes being made in the silver mines.

On a chilly day in December Mark set out for Humboldt County, known as "the richest mineral region upon God's footstool." He had three companions, Ballou, a blacksmith of sixty, and two young lawyers. They took about 1,800 pounds of provisions and mining tools. Two weeks later, in a driving snow, they reached Unionville in the Humboldt.

Unionville had a Liberty Pole and eleven cabins on both sides of a canyon. The newcomers erected a rude cabin for themselves, and roofed it with canvas, leaving an open corner for a chimney. Then they were ready to go get their fortune. The first day out, Mark scooped up some glistening stones and thought his search was over. The more experienced Ballou dismissed his find as granite and mica not worth ten cents an acre. After many more days of digging, Ballou broke off some fragments of clean white rock with a hammer and exposed a ragged thread of blue. He said that the thread was silver, mixed with baser metals.

They set up claims for 300 feet each. Mark's enthusiasm dimmed when Ballou said their ledge might go hundreds of feet deep, and that even when they got the ore out, they would have to haul it to the silver mill for the costly process of extracting the silver. They set to work to sink a shaft. Loose stones near the surface soon gave way to solid rock that blasting powder alone could budge. In a week they had dug barely twelve feet. Then they tried tunneling in from the side. In another week they had a tunnel about big enough for a hogshead. Mark Twain quit for good.

On the hazardous journey back to Carson City, his adventures included being caught in a flood and lost in a snowstorm. His heart was set on trying his luck at the Esmeralda, another renowned silver region. His savings were exhausted but Orion staked him.

In the Esmeralda mining town of Aurora, Mark shared a cabin with a big, good-natured man named Calvin Higbie. They took up several claims but none yielded more than the price the mills charged for working the ore. When flour rose to a dollar a pound and Orion's stake was gone, Mark went to work with a shovel in a quartz mill. At the end of a week, overcome by the "exceeding hardness of the labor," he gave notice. The employer protested that Mark was getting the good round sum of $10 a week. What more did he want? Mark proposed about $400,000 a month—and board.

They forgot their hardships at the frontier dance hall. Higbie recalled later that Mark was always the life of the party. Sometimes he would do a hoedown or a double-shuffle alone, talking to himself, while others stood around and watched him "too full of mirth to dance." Women were always eager to have him for a partner.

News spread that the Wide West Company had suddenly struck it rich. Calvin Higbie waited in ambush for two days so he could descend the Wide West shaft unobserved. He returned to their cabin in a state of smothered excitement. He'd found their ore came from a blind lead, he told Mark. It was theirs for the taking.

A blind lead was a ledge that did not crop out above the surface and could be discovered only by chance. Higbie had had a hunch that Wide West's new ore did not come from the Wide West vein. Down in the shaft he had discovered that the blind lead cut through the Wide West vein, but continued its own way, enclosed in its own casing of rocks and clay. It was thus public property.

Feeling the need of an influential friend, they invited the Wide West foreman, a man named Allen, to be their partner. The three of them made a claim on the blind lead in their three names, for 600 feet in all. Thus they could forbid the Wide West to take any more ore from their blind lead vein. All that night they talked about how they were going to spend their huge wealth.

By local law, the claimant of a ledge would forfeit his claim if he did not do a certain amount of mining within ten days. Mark planned to start digging at once, but early the next morning someone brought word that a friend of his who was staying out in the country was sick and needed help. He left a note at the cabin for Higbie, saying he would be back as soon as possible. Then he took off.

It was nine days before his friend was well enough

to be left alone. Mark reached his cabin just before midnight of the tenth day. When he opened the door, he saw Higbie sitting motionless by the light of a tallow candle. He was staring at the note that Mark had left him, reading it for the first time!

Higbie had left the same day Mark did to follow up a lead at Mono Lake—and had tossed a note in the window for Mark.

Nor had Allen worked their claim. Mark heard that a telegram had called him to California but in any case was back in time to take a share in the new ownership of the blind lead claim. Higbie and Mark Twain lost out completely, but nothing could take away from them their joy of feeling like millionaires for ten days.

For some time, unknown to his rugged and mostly illiterate companions, Mark had been writing humorous letters to the *Territorial Enterprise* in Virginia City, signing himself "Josh." Some of them were printed. Not long after the blind lead fiasco he received a letter from the *Enterprise,* offering him a job for $25 a week. In July 1862, he set out on a 130 mile hike to Virginia City.

On a hot August day, a heavily bearded man, slight in stature, dressed in a blue woolen shirt, his pants stuffed in his boots, a revolver slung to his belt, walked into the *Enterprise* office.

"My name is Clemens, and I've come to write for the paper," he said.

5

wild humorist of the pacific slope

Training is everything. The peach was once a bitter almond; cauliflower is nothing but cabbage with a college education.

—Mark Twain, quoting
Pudd'nhead Wilson's Calendar

Virginia City was another Carson City but wilder and larger, with a population approaching 18,000, and built on the side of a mountain. Beneath it stretched the incredibly rich Comstock Lode. As in

Carson City, everyone hoped to become a millionaire and some did.

Joseph T. Goodman, editor of the *Territorial Enterprise*, built the paper up from a dying journal to a great daily with five editors and twenty-three compositors, selling at a subscription price of $16 a year and with exorbitant advertising rates. His only advice to his new reporter was to omit "it is rumored" in his stories and always get the facts, but he did not try to curb Mark Twain's wild imagination, which produced hoaxes such as appeared in an October 1862 issue. This was his story about the discovery of a petrified man, the most puzzling thing about him being that he was in the act of thumbing his nose. To Mark's disgust, his readers accepted his "string of roaring absurdities" about the petrified man "in innocent good faith."

His salary was soon raised to $40 weekly, paid in two $20 gold pieces. In addition, miners were constantly giving him stock in this and that claim if he so much as mentioned that claim in a story. He did not have to say that it was good. It was enough to say that a ledge was "six feet wide" or that its rock "resembled the Comstock" (as most rock did), or that the shaft had a new wire rope or force pump.

It was not unusual for men to hand him stock for so many feet in their mines, expecting nothing in return. He could have made a killing several times, if he had been at the right place at the right time to accept these donations. He did acquire a trunk full of stock which he figured should be good for something, sometime. Men were being turned into nabobs overnight. One of them wore $6,000 diamonds and was wretched because he could not spend money as fast as he made it.

In the midst of Virginia City's gambling dens, saloons, brothels, and jails, a literary paper called the *Weekly Occidental* was hopefully born. It actually ran a serialized novel, one chapter being contributed each week by a different member of the staff, including the editor's wife. Before its early death, it carried a long poem by Samuel Clemens (he called it doggerel), *The Aged Pilot Man.*

Once a year he went back to Carson City to report on legislative procedures for the *Enterprise.* This gave him his first taste of political manipulations, which he found both funny and disgusting. The legislature levied taxes of between $30,000 and $40,000, then ordered expenditures of a million. During the sixty days they sat, they granted so many private toll-road franchises that Mark Twain wondered if Congress should not enlarge the Territory to make room for them. His heavily ironic letters to the *Enterprise* were signed "Mark Twain," the first recorded use of this pseudonym in his writing.

Nevada became a state in 1864. Governor Nye was easily elected its first senator. Gentle, unworldly, Orion might have been Secretary of State but just before nomination day he switched from a lenient attitude toward whisky to total teetotalism. He did not get a single vote. The rest of his life was one failure after another.

Artemus Ward, the humorist, stopped in Virginia City in December 1863 on a nationwide lecture tour. Mark Twain, Joe Goodman, and others of the *Enterprise* staff welcomed him in a celebration that lasted twelve days. He is little read today because of his dependence on dialect and misspellings. As a lecturer he was an expert at making people laugh. Mark Twain may well have studied his techniques. Ward was already doomed at the time of this splendid celebration; he would die three years later of tuberculosis.

In May 1864, Mark Twain left Virginia City by stagecoach for San Francisco. One cause given for his abrupt departure was a joke in the *Enterprise* that miscarried and caused the victim of it to threaten him with a duel. Anyway he was curious about San Francisco.

From the sale of a few of his stock certificates he was able to live a "butterfly" existence in the city's best hotel, which lasted until the bottom fell out of the stock market. He threw the rest of his useless stock certificates away, moved to a boarding house, and got a job on the *Morning Call,* with Steve Gillis, a fellow exile from Virginia City.

Along with routine and often dull reporting, he wrote articles about local corruption among police and politicians and about the brutal treatment doled out to the Chinese population. When his stories were too strong a dose for the conservative *Call*, he sent them to *The Golden Era*, which had published sketches he sent from Virginia City, or to *The Californian*, another literary publication.

Everything about San Francisco pleased him, its old-fashioned architecture, its mild climate, the brilliance of the calla lillies, geraniums, and other flowers usually grown in pots but which flourished outdoors here all year round. The city's main appeal to him was its Bohemian life of young intellectuals, newspapermen, poets, writers. One of the latter was Bret Harte, former schoolmaster, a year younger than Mark Twain, but more advanced in writing techniques. In later years Mark Twain would become furious with Bret Harte for reasons to be mentioned later, but he always credited him with rubbing the rough edges from his writing and thus making it presentable to the critics.

The *Morning Call* asked him to resign on one excuse or another. In his *Autobiography*, Mark Twain would boast that he finally got his revenge; the *Call* building was reduced to a skeleton in the great fire and earthquake of 1906. *The Californian* languished and was sold to a rich man who let it die.

Out of funds and out of jobs, Mark Twain let himself be talked into trying pocket mining for gold in the Sacramento Valley. A pocket mine is a pocket of gold in one spot. A man who finds a pocket mine may take out several thousand dollars in one shovel. Mark Twain wandered for three months in the

47

pocket mining region of Angel's Camp, Calaveras County, carrying on his shoulder pans and shovels and sleeping under trees or in the huts of hospitable miners. He did not find a trace of gold. This ended his mining days, in which luck had been so noticeably missing.

He got something else from Angel's Camp—a story about a man who had a jumping frog, and how he bet a stranger that his frog could outjump any other frog, and how the stranger stuffed the frog so full of quail shot it could not jump at all. Back in San Francisco, he wrote the story up. The New York *Saturday Press* published it in November 1865 under the title of "Jim Smiley and his Jumping Frog." (A later title was "The Notorious Frog of Calaveras County.") The story was reprinted elsewhere. Some Mark Twain fans do not care for it. What is so funny about a frog being mistreated? At the time people all over the country got a laugh out of it. Overnight "the wild humorist of the Pacific Slope" was famous. Personally Mark Twain was little impressed with a fame based on a backwoods tale that was not even his own.

In March 1866, he set sail for the Sandwich Islands, as Hawaii was then called, under the auspices of the Sacramento *Union,* who were paying his fare and a fixed sum for each of his travel letters. He fell quickly under the spell of the tropical islands and wrote about them with the fresh vision of one newly initiated into the Garden of Eden. During his five-

48

month stay, he traveled all over them, studied the history and customs of the people, and came to the reluctant conclusion that while the ancient rulers had been far from perfect, the people had gained little and lost much from their contact with white people, especially the missionaries who made them wear calico dresses, bonnets, and stovepipe hats and banned their gala festivals and hula hula dances. He never was able to revisit Hawaii, but he did not forget its charm.

In the summer of 1866, he was back in San Francisco, as "centless" as the Last Rose of Summer, to quote one of his worser puns. A former editor encouraged him to give a public lecture on the Sandwich Islands. On credit he rented the new opera house for $50 and invested $150 in advertising. Posters announced: "Doors open at 7½. The trouble will begin at 8."

In advance he was in torture, but he found himself speaking to a full house. People laughed at everything, even the serious parts. Newspapers were kind. He gave more lectures in California and Nevada, always finding an eager reception. His audiences were not blasé; they welcomed any entertainment.

From home he had bad news. Pamela's husband, Will Moffett, had died; she was living with his mother. He decided it was time to go back to the States. (California was still not considered part of the United States.) He chose a long way home.

On December 15, 1866, he left on a steamboat which sailed along the Mexican coast to San Juan del Sur, in Nicaragua. The journey was enriched by his acquaintance with Captain Ned Wakeman, a Connecticut Yankee. His colorful language and enormous repertory of stories won Mark Twain over completely. Ned Wakeman in one form or another popped up repeatedly in his future writings.

The rest of the trip assumed aspects of a nightmare. There was, as yet, no Panama Canal. Passengers crossed the Isthmus jungle by mule, wagon, and boat, to meet the steamer *San Francisco* on the Atlantic side. Cholera struck their first day out to sea and spread rapidly from steerage to first-class passengers. Every day sea burial services were held for the shrouded victims. The *San Francisco* reached New York on January 12, 1867. So the ship would not be quarantined, the sick were listed as suffering from dropsy. On a diet of brandy, Mark Twain stayed healthy.

6

the innocents of the quaker city

Who has not heard of him? Who has not laughed over his quaint sayings and queer ideas? Who has not fairly succumbed to his racy anecdotes and melted under his pathetic stories?

—publisher's blurb for *The Innocents Abroad*

An advertisement in a New York paper announced a pleasure cruise to Europe and the Holy Land on the ship *Quaker City*. The cruise was organized by the well-known Reverend Henry Ward Beecher. General Sherman was expected to go along. Prospective passengers were required to give character references. The round trip fare was $1,250, insuring that all would be at least moderately prosperous. Mark Twain suggested to the *Alta Californian* that they sponsor him as they had done on his journey in the Sandwich Islands. Eventually they agreed to pay his fare plus $20 for each newsletter sent back.

Since his return from California, he had been writing for the *Alta* about New York life. To gather material he visited theaters, ballet performances, dance halls, and Barnum's Museum. He had even traipsed over to the Plymouth Church to hear Reverend Henry Ward Beecher preach. Beecher was a plain, unimpressive man offstage, but his voice was rich and resonant and he held his parishioners spellbound. It occurred to Mark Twain that he should be an actor. From him, he learned the value of a pause to keep your audience in suspense.

In March 1867 he made a quick trip to St. Louis to see his mother, his widowed sister Pamela, and her two children. Pamela lectured him, as was her habit, on his intemperance, his extravagance, and his habit of joking about sacred matters. Possibly in reaction to her nagging, he wrote an anti-female suffrage article for the Missouri *Democrat,* in which he asserted that no woman would ever go to the polls because she would have to tell her age.

In St. Louis, he gave his lecture on the Sandwich Islands, mixing poetic descriptions of volcanoes in eruption with history and funny anecdotes. At one point, he promised to show how cannibalism was practiced in the islands if some lady would kindly volunteer an infant for the occasion! In Hannibal, where bad times had come since the railroads had taken over much of the river traffic, he gave a similar lecture. He lectured in Quincy, Illinois, and in Keokuk, and then returned to New York.

His first New York lecture took place on May 6, at Cooper Union. Though he had to compete with a troupe of Japanese acrobats, Frank Fuller, his sponsor and friend, produced a full hall by giving free tickets to schoolteachers. The New York *Tribune* gave him an excellent review. The lecture was a success every way but financially.

In that same month his first book was published, *The Celebrated Jumping Frog, and Other Sketches.* His editor and publisher was a San Francisco friend, C. H. Webb. The book had a modest sale but he never was able to collect royalties.

The *Quaker City* sailed from a Wall Street pier on June 8. Neither Reverend Beecher nor General Sherman were among its seventy-five passengers. Mark Twain was the nearest to a celebrity aboard. The passenger list included an assortment of doctors, professors, and ministers of the gospel. One of these asked Captain Duncan if he could halt the expedition on Sundays. Duncan was a former Sunday School Superintendent and no expert in profanity like Ned Wakeman, but he was, after all, a seaman. He told the minister that he had no intention of anchoring in the middle of the Atlantic.

Mark Twain did find two sympathetic souls. One was his roommate, Dan Slote, a plump and balding man who owned a stationery firm. He smoked, was not adverse to sharing Mark's champagne, and did not preach at him. Another shipboard friend was Mrs. Mary Mason Fairbanks, who was also writing newspaper articles about the cruise, for her husband's newspaper, the Cleveland *Herald*. She mothered Mark Twain, sewed on his buttons, gave him social hints. He even allowed her to censure his newsletters, blotting out anything she considered bad taste. Gradually he struck up acquaintance with some of the younger men on board, who had not lived long enough to grow stuffy.

But as far as the rest of the passengers were concerned, Mark Twain was out of his element. He must have yearned at times for the rough companionship of his river pilots, or prospectors, or the outlaws of Hannibal. Shipboard life, as he summed it up, was composed of decorum, dinner, and dominoes.

He himself was not yet free of the disease of American snobbery, the nature of which is to hold everything foreign as either contemptible or ridiculous. In the Azores, their first stop, he described the poverty-stricken Portuguese inhabitants as "vermin," for which he would later try to make amends. The

difference between him and others with the same
malady was that he outgrew his prejudices, at least
most of them.

At Marseilles, the pilgrims, as he dubbed his fellow passengers, took a train to Paris. There he visited
the Louvre art museum, the Cathedral of Notre
Dame, the morgue, the poor section of Faubourg St.
Antoine, home of "the people who start the revolu-
tions," and watched the can-can dancers in a night-
club, all adding up to "a gorgeous time," as he wrote
home.

The passengers rejoined their ship at Marseilles
and they sailed to Italy. From Florence he commented that the Arno might be a plausible river if
some water was dumped in it. He wrote of lovely
Venice "drowsing" in the sunset mist. "Drowsing"
was one of his favorite words. He visited Pompeii
and climbed Vesuvius; Mrs. Fairbanks edited out
of his newsletter a description of how a woman in
hoopskirts looked from behind as she climbed the
volcano. In Rome he wrote of the irony that Romans
should have thrown Christians to the wild beasts in
the Coliseum, but that when Christians came to
power they developed the thumbscrew for the In-
quisition.

Italy was "one vast museum." Old Masters left
him unimpressed. He grew weary of saints and
martyrs and said that 13,000 St. Jeromes, 22,000 St.
Marks, 16,000 St. Matthews, 60,000 St. Sebastians

were just a few too many. His levity about great art did not amuse everybody.

One day the *Quaker City* skirted the gray and brown isles of Greece, then anchored in the ancient harbor of Piraeus. By telescope they could glimpse the Parthenon but because of a rigid quarantine were not allowed to land. Late that night, Mark and three others went ashore in a small boat and stealthily made their way to the immortal temple—an adventure rivalling some of those of his boyhood.

Turkey was a disappointment. The famous mosque of Santa Sophia in Constantinople struck him as dingy and gloomy. Beggars were the only thing in which Turkey excelled, he insisted. He saw a three-legged woman, a seven-fingered dwarf, and a man with an eye in his cheek.

They reached Russia. Sevastopol was still largely in ruins from the Crimean War. Though the Russians were reputed to be suspicious, Mark passed easily through customs on a borrowed passport, having misplaced his own. Odessa, their next stop, had the air of an American city, with its wide streets lined with acacias.

In Yalta, they were invited, on August 26, 1867, to visit Emperor Alexander I, acclaimed in America for setting the Russian serfs free. Royal carriages brought the *Quaker City* passengers to the palace. Alexander and his empress, who both spoke English, received them graciously. Mark Twain was admittedly rather awed by this, his first brush with royalty, and impressed that they seemed "strangely like common mortals."

From Russia, they sailed to the Holy Land, the Middle East. Their first Asian stop was Smyrna. That was where a young passenger named Charles Langdon, son of an Elmira, New York, coal magnate, showed Mark Twain a miniature of his sister Olivia, a dark-haired beauty. Mark fell in love at the sight of it.

In the next weeks the *Quaker City* passengers visited scores of places familiar by name to Biblical scholars. For a month they traveled through Palestine on horseback. Mark Twain noted that they made an odd sight with their white umbrellas, thick green spectacles, elbows flapping as they bounded along on their mounts. For camping out, native Arabians provided them with carpeted tents, iron bedsteads, white sheets and blankets, white tablecloths and silverware, lavish meals of mutton, chicken, and goose—all for five dollars a day in gold.

Mark had often mocked the pious hypocrisy of some of the passengers; he was furious when they spurred on their horses for thirteen straight hours to reach Damascus on Saturday night instead of the Sabbath. If they had wanted to prove themselves Christians, they would have done better to show some mercy for their suffering animals.

Stepping on sacred toes bothered him not at all.

57

He dismissed the Dead Sea as a fraud. When a boatman overcharged them to sail on the Sea of Galilee, he said he knew why Christ walked. But he felt compassion for the Syrian people as he had not for the Portuguese in the Azores, desperately poor as they were, and ground down by a system of taxation that would have driven any other nation frantic.

After "dismal, smileless Palestine," beautiful Egypt could not hold them. "We merely glanced at it and were ready for home." The *Quaker City* sailed into New York harbor on November 19, 1867. The pilgrims disembarked with their myriads of souvenirs, bits of monuments and marble columns, plaster from mosques and churches, and some bones collected in Sevastopol, which their proud owner was convinced were parts of a general.

In the course of the voyage, Mark found time to send 53 newsletters to the *Alta Californian*, three to the New York *Herald* and six to the New York *Tribune*. In a final piece for the *Herald*, he wrote that people of the places they had toured would remember that Americans talked loudly, that they watched their expenses carefully, and that they made the natives feel rather small by bearing "down on them with America's greatness." This was certainly one of the earliest critiques of the American tourist.

Unknown to him, his articles were creating a sensation. There had never been anything like them. In Hartford, Connecticut, Elisha Bliss, editor and owner of the American Publishing Company, a subscription house, read some of them, reflected that there might be a book in them, and resolved to write their author as soon as he returned. This was the germ of an idea from which Mark Twain's *The Innocents Abroad,* his first popular success, was born.

7

*love, courtship,
marriage, success*

There is no unhappiness like the misery of sighting land
(and work) again after a cheerful, careless voyage.
—Mark Twain

Soon after his return, Mark Twain went to Washington to work as private secretary to Senator William
M. Stewart. The senator had been champion to the
miners in Nevada, where Mark had first known him.
Now he was rich and respectable and displeased by
his secretary's penchant for big cigars and ironic
comments. Mark Twain lasted only long enough to

get material for a burlesque sketch: "My Late Senatorial Secretaryship."

He stayed on in Washington as correspondent for the New York *Tribune* and other journals, and to write for a literary monthly called *Galaxy*. His total earnings gave him a bare living; he stayed in a series of grubby boarding houses. The most valuable part of his Washington experience was that he had a chance to learn about the underside of the capital's political life. At this time it did not present a pretty picture and led to his much-quoted remark that there was no distinctly native American criminal class except Congress.

On December 1, 1867, he received the letter from Elisha Bliss, forwarded from New York, suggesting a book about the *Quaker City*. What interested Mark Twain was that Bliss' American Publishing Company was a subscription house.

Subscription houses distributed books not through bookstores but by door-to-door salesmen who traveled all over the country even to the most remote villages and farms. Most of their subscribers had never been near a bookstore. Subscription books had to be long because bulky books sold best. They had to have a gaudy cover and many illustrations. In fact engravings were often used over and over in different books, even though they bore scant relation to the text. Literary critics rarely bothered to review subscription books. It was said that a writer who sold his books by subscriptions lost caste. The fact remained that they outsold, by far, books sold through bookstores.

The matter of losing caste did not worry Mark Twain. The feeble sales of *Jumping Frog* had wounded him. What he wanted now was to earn money by writing. He answered Elisha Bliss at once and in January 1868, he went to Hartford to see him. The deal was made. Mark promised to deliver a book of some 240,000 words, based on his *Alta* letters, in return for a 5 percent royalty on the subscription price.

During his brief stay in Hartford, he was the guest of John Hooker and his wife, Isabella Beecher Hooker, a formidable woman who was the sister of Reverend Henry Ward Beecher. To Mrs. Fairbanks, Mark wrote that in their house he did not dare smoke or do anything else comfortable. Yet he was enchanted with Hartford, which he described as a city without poverty, without saloons, and, so far as he could tell, a city where no one swore.

Mrs. Fairbanks, who was concerned about his welfare, wrote back that what he needed was a good wife to stabilize him. "I want a good wife," he quipped, "two of them if they are particularly good —but where is the wherewithal?" He could, as yet, barely support himself.

The truth was that Mrs. Fairbanks was echoing his own thoughts.

Before going to Hartford, on December 27, 1867, to be exact, his young friend of the *Quaker City,*

Charles Langdon, had invited him to the St. Nicholas Hotel in New York City to meet his parents and his sister Olivia. Mark found her to be no less beautiful in real life than in the miniature Charlie had shown him. On New Year's Eve, he took her to a reading by Charles Dickens. He was disappointed in Dickens, who spoke in a monotone, but he was enraptured by his companion, who was then twenty-two and "sweet and timid and lovely."

The Langdons asked him to visit them in Elmira. He did not immediately take advantage of their invitation. For one thing, he had to go to San Francisco to convince the *Alta* that he, not they, had the rights to his *Quaker City* letters, on which, with considerable rewriting, his book for Bliss would be based. He saw old friends while he was there, including Bret Harte, now editor of the *Overland Monthly*, and he gave a lecture on Venice.

The crowded halls and the applause that always greeted his lectures made it clear that, for him, public speaking could be rather more lucrative than reporting. On his return from California, he signed up with James Redpath, one of the first lecture agents, and a maverick in his own right, who believed in bringing culture to the masses and fought for the civil rights of black people.

For a fee of 10 percent, Redpath arranged speaking tours, made up a schedule, took care of hotel accommodations and all the tasks of travel which, formerly, even famous persons like Ralph Waldo

Emerson had had to do on their own. Under Redpath's tutelage, Mark Twain became known as a person and a performer from coast to coast.

He was superb at gauging his audience, at judging how to get a laugh, or a gasp of shocked giggles. When he switched to giving readings, like Dickens, of his own works, he rewrote the material completely; what was effective on the printed page was not necessarily good theatre on the stage. A perfectionist, he wrote all his speeches in advance, and then delivered them as though they were impromptu. He enjoyed his mastery of a different technique but did not enjoy the life of one-night stands, of lonely hotel rooms, or what was sometimes even worse, being the overnight guest in homes where he could not feel at his ease. What made him most impatient was that he saw himself being pushed into the category of a buffoon, a clown, whose job was simply to amuse. He did not want his life's work to be limited to that.

Between lecturing and writing, he did not get to Elmira to see Olivia until August 1868, soon after he had delivered the manuscript of *The Innocents Abroad* to Elisha Bliss. He knew the Langdons were not poor, but he was hardly prepared for their huge brownstone mansion at 21 Main Street, with grounds covering a city block. When he passed through the three sets of iron gates and entered vast rooms filled with heavy mahogany furniture and darkened by rich heavy drapes, he was entering a foreign world.

During the Civil War, Jervis Langdon, Olivia's father, had gained his wealth by setting up a coal and iron monopoly around Buffalo and Elmira, convenient to Pennsylvania's anthracite mines. For an industrialist he had redeeming qualities. He had helped fugitive slaves even before the war and was now aiding freed slaves and supporting Negro education. Of his three children—Charles, Susan, and Olivia—Livy, as the family called her, was his favorite.

At sixteen she had injured her spine and for two years had lain in her bedroom, paralyzed. In despair, her parents had called in a "mind healer" named Dr. Newton. He entered her room, opened the window and drapes, and told her she was going to walk a few steps. She obeyed him and from then on was able to walk unaided, though never more than 200 yards or so without a rest. Dr. Newton later told Mark Twain he thought he had achieved this miracle by electricity.

Mark spent several weeks in the Langdon home, not guessing he might be wearing out his welcome. Livy disapproved of his swearing, drinking, and smoking, and he promised to reform. To please her he went to church to listen to the Reverend Thomas K. Beecher, brother of Isabella and Henry Ward Beecher. In the glow of Mark's love, everything Livy believed was right. He felt himself a hopeless sinner. She refused to listen to talk of his love, but agreed to a brother-sister relationship.

A month or so later he paid another visit. He was only invited to stay overnight. Due to an accident on the way to the station he had to be brought back. His injuries were slight; he played sick for another couple of days just to enjoy the luxury of having Livy nurse him.

After he left, he wrote her from Hartford, where he was working on revisions of *The Innocents Abroad* with Elisha Bliss, telling her of a new friend, the Reverend Joseph Hopkins Twichell, pastor of the Asylum Hill Congregational Church of Hartford. Such a friendship must have relieved Livy of some of her doubts about the barbarian who was pushing his way into her life. In truth, Twichell was an unorthodox minister, handsome, athletic, outgoing, tolerant, not at all like the bluenoses on the *Quaker City*. Mark Twain's brand of humor delighted him.

Mark visited the Langdons for the third time on November 21. He felt enough at home to walk in unannounced, saying that the prodigal had returned and could he have some breakfast. Redpath had arranged for him to give a lecture in Elmira, which Livy attended. That night he told her he could no longer pretend that his feelings for her were brotherly. For six days he used all his arts of persuasion. She finally admitted she loved him.

Her parents did not forbid their engagement but asked Mark to draw up a list of character references. They wanted to learn more about this Mr. Clemens. He gave them names and addresses. Mrs. Fairbanks was almost the only one to say something good about him. A bank cashier prophesied that he would fill a drunkard's grave. A San Francisco clergyman called him a humbug. Other reports were worse.

"Haven't you a friend in the world?" Mr. Langdon asked him.

"Apparently not," Mark said. He did not confess that he had omitted the names of his real friends, like Joe Goodman of the Virginia City *Enterprise*.

"I'll be your friend myself," Langdon said, surprisingly. To his credit, he never hinted that Mark Twain wanted to marry Livy for her money.

In his writing, Mark Twain was becoming more and more outspoken. In *Packard's Monthly* of March 1869, he published a satire called "Open Letter to Commodore Vanderbilt," telling the Commodore he had yet to hear of anything he had done which was not shameful and urging him to surprise everyone by doing something right. He would have a great deal to say in the future, in a mixture of irony and anger, about America's ruling class of financiers.

Paradoxically, Mark Twain's own dominant desire now was to make enough money so Livy would not have to change her way of living. His lectures that season paid him nearly $9,000. Langdon wanted him in a more stable business and gave him a loan so that he could buy a part interest in the Buffalo *Express*. Mark accepted with reservations.

The Innocents Abroad was published in the fall of 1869. Bliss advertised it as "The Most Unique and Spicy Volume in Existence." An army of book salesmen canvassed the country, getting advance orders. By the end of the year more than 30,000 copies had been sold. The book was waltzing him out of debt, Mark Twain commented gleefully. Breaking tradition, a few literary critics mentioned it. William Dean Howells of the *Atlantic Monthly* praised it highly; he would become another lifelong friend of Mark's. Oliver Wendell Holmes wrote him a flattering letter.

In the meantime he was supplying the Buffalo *Express* with short columns about his adventures in the West. These would be the basis for his next book, *Roughing It*.

Samuel L. Clemens and Olivia Langdon were married in the Langdon parlor on February 2, 1870. Reverend Thomas K. Beecher of Elmira and Reverend Joseph Twichell of Hartford performed the ceremony jointly. Mark's mother refused to leave St. Louis but sent Pamela and her daughter Annie. Mrs. Fairbanks attended, as did the many friends and relatives of the Langdons.

The wedding guests accompanied the young couple in a private railroad car to Buffalo but at the station they were sent off alone in a sleigh, to what Mark Twain thought would be the boarding house an employee of Langdon was to select for him. The sleigh driver stopped in front of a brightly lit three-story brick mansion in a fashionable district—472 Delaware Avenue. It did not look like a boarding house to Mark. The mystery was soon explained. Jervis Langdon met them at the door with the deed to the house and a check for its maintenance. This was his wedding gift.

Livy had been in on the secret and had chosen the furniture. The wedding guests followed them as Mark went from the scarlet study to the blue satin drawing room. It seemed to this once barefoot boy of Hannibal that he had stepped into an enchanted palace.

Servants came with the house. When the guests had gone, the Irish coachman, Patrick McAleer, appeared to inquire what their needs for the next day would be. Ellen, the Irish cook, came to get orders for the morning's marketing. Her face broke into smiles when Mark told her that neither of them knew whether beefsteak was sold by the barrel or the yard.

The next weeks, in his words, were "burdened and bent with happiness." He rarely went to the *Express* office. Breakfast was at ten. They ate dinner alone at a table covered with a fringed red cloth. In the evenings he read poetry to his wife.

The beautiful girl he had worshipped from afar proved to be a tender and affectionate companion with a natural grace and dignity that won over everybody. While Mark had promised to change his ways to please her, in the end it was Livy who did most of the changing. She stopped objecting to his cigars and his drinking and sometimes took a drink herself. She stopped pressing him to go to church and over the years became less strict herself about religious ceremonies. The one thing she did not like was his swearing.

Once she heard him in the bathroom next to their bedroom cursing because of some missing shirt button. He had not realized the door between the rooms was open. Seeing Livy lying on their bed, her eyes flashing dangerously, he started to apologize. She interrupted him, and in her sweetly modulated voice repeated word for word what he had said. It sounded so funny they both burst out laughing and could not stop.

8

community living at
nook farm

A man's got to be in his own heaven to be happy.
— Mark Twain in *Extract from Captain
Stormfield's Visit to Heaven*

Sorrow crept into their paradise the first year of
marriage. Jervis Langdon died of cancer in August
1870, a dreadful blow to Livy. That November, she
gave birth to a son but he was a sickly baby who lived
only twenty-two months. Livy herself fell seriously
ill.

Mark Twain, harassed and gloomy, plunged into his duties at the Buffalo *Express*. He trained reporters to omit slang and adjectives. Editorials were his department. He did one virulent attack on lynching in the South. He endorsed the fight of Frederick Douglass against segregation in the schools. In an article for the monthly, *Galaxy*, he berated a minister who had urged workmen to keep out of fashionable church pews because "common people did not smell good." There was reason to believe, Mark Twain wrote, that there might be working people in heaven—also Negroes, Eskimos, Arabs, Indians, maybe some Spaniards and Portuguese. Later he reflected that some of the "humor" he wrote in this period could have been injected into a funeral "without disturbing the solemnity of the occasion."

It was true that he was also trying to find time to work on his new book *Roughing It*, for which Bliss had given him a contract and upped his royalty to 7½ percent of the subscription price. *Roughing It* was the story of his adventures in the West from the time he and Orion left in a stagecoach through his Sandwich Islands journey, and to make it as long as Bliss demanded, he was cramming it full of all the humorous anecdotes he had heard in those years.

But Buffalo had become tangled in his consciousness with Livy's sickness and sorrow. He sold out his interest in the *Express,* and in October of 1872, moved his family to Hartford, Connecticut. John and Isabella Hooker, with whom he had stayed on his first visit, were away; he rented their house in Nook Farm, a community in western Hartford.

The estate of Nook Farm had originally belonged to John Hooker. He sold it off to relatives and friends of kindred intellectual and cultural interests. Their politics were mostly liberal. Isabella Hooker, who Mark Twain at first found so intimidating, became a leading suffragette. Nook Farm retained a delightfully unconventional atmosphere. No one locked doors. Paths were worn between houses of neighbors calling on each other. They entered without knocking, often in slippers and negligee.

Several Nook Farm inhabitants had written a book or so. The only really famous one before Mark Twain came was Harriet Beecher Stowe, another of the remarkable Beecher family, and author of *Uncle Tom's Cabin*. Calvin Stowe, her husband, was a retired professor. Harriet had kept on writing, too much and too fast some said, to support the family. In her old age she became a child again and spent her time gathering wildflowers which she brought to her sister Isabella or to Livy.

Mark Twain's boon companion, Reverend Joseph Twichell, with his wife, were part of the Nook Farm community. His other closest friends those first years were Charles Dudley Warner and his wife, Susan. Warner, a co-owner of the Hartford *Courant*, would be remembered for a charming little volume,

My Summer in a Garden—and for a not-too-success-
ful collaboration with Mark Twain.

Both *The Innocents Abroad* and the recently published *Roughing It* were in the category of nonfiction, albeit humorous nonfiction. Mark had never
tried his hand at long fiction. One night when the
Warners and the Clemens were having dinner together, Mark and Warner fell to talking about the
stupidity of modern novels. Their wives urged them
to write a novel themselves, a challenge they could
not resist.

They began early in 1873. Each evening the two
men read aloud what they had written that day.
Their wives made suggestions. The manuscript was
finished in about three months and was published
by Bliss in December 1873 as *The Gilded Age*. About
35,000 copies were sold the first two months but
then sales fell off.

Warner's part of the novel dealt with a young
man, Phil Sterling, who went west to make a fortune
so that he could marry a rich girl, and finally did
find a mountain of coal, after which everyone hung
on his slightest word as though it was "solid wisdom."

To anyone who asked him, Mark Twain could
reel off the chapters of *The Gilded Age* that were his
own. His part was an exposé of corrupt Washington,
as it had never been exposed before. His unctious
Congressman Dilworthy, who could never resist a
bribe, was a near replica of the notorious congressman Samuel Pomeroy—whom Mark had met. His

74

female protagonist, Laura Hawkins (named after his childhood sweetheart) was the first woman lobbyist in American literature; she used both feminine wiles and blackmail to get what she wanted.

The most notable character was Colonel Sellers, a relic of Southern gentry, who is trying to sell an inherited property of 100,000 acres (like the Tennessee property of Mark's father) to the government at an immense profit but is foiled at every turn. In the face of dire adversity, the Colonel never loses hope that millions were around the corner.

Sellers was based on a relative of Mark Twain, James Lampton. In a tragicomic scene, an unexpected guest arrives at his home at dinnertime and is given raw turnips and nothing else. Sellers insists they are a rare imported variety of such subtle taste that it would be criminal to serve them with any drink but pure water! Mark Twain has claimed that the turnip banquet actually took place; he was Lampton's unexpected guest.

All in all, *The Gilded Age* was a disjointed novel, with some excellent scenes. The last part, beginning where Laura Hawkins murders the lover who had betrayed her, is rank melodrama. It was and is important because of its realistic portrait of Washington in the 1870s and because it set a precedent in America of fiction played against a background of current affairs, in contrast to the namby pamby romances of the period.

In September 1874, Mark Twain moved into his

own Nook Farm house, at 351 Farmington Avenue —he, Livy, their two-year-old daughter, Olivia Susan (born March 19, 1872) and the baby, Clara, born the previous June 8. There were still workmen around; nothing was really finished.

Mark Twain had bought five acres of land two years before and hired an architect to build the house to his own specifications. There was nothing else like it in Hartford. It is now a museum and there is still nothing like it.

It had nineteen rooms, five bathrooms with indoor plumbing which was then a novelty, a porch like a riverboat, a balcony like a pilot house, turrets like a medieval castle, and a host of chimneys. Every room had its fireplace and mantelpieces inlaid and carved with gargoyles, cherubs, and sphinxes. The dining room fireplace had a window above the mantel and the flue diverted to both sides, so that in wintertime guests could watch the flames and snowflakes above them. Over the mantel in the library was a quotation from Emerson: "The ornament of a house is the friends who frequent it." The library opened onto a large glass conservatory which had a fountain; vines flowered and calla lilies bloomed in the coldest weather.

Eventually the mansion was largely furnished with antiques and works of art which Mark and Livy brought back from Europe, adding to its already large cost.

Mark Twain's luxurious study was on the second

floor. He seldom used it; it was turned into a school-room for his children. Sometimes he tried to write in the third-floor billiard room, or in the room above the stable. On occasion he went over to Reverend Twichell's house, thinking he could concentrate better there.

To look after the mammoth establishment on Farmington Avenue, they kept an average of six servants—nursemaid, cook, butler, housemaid, laundress, coachman.

The house became a center for various cultural and intellectual gatherings. A Browning Society met once a week in the billiard room to listen to Mark Twain reading Browning's poetry. Young girls came to a Saturday Morning Club for "cultural and social training." Men of the community had a Friday Evening Club. Women were tolerated only if they kept silent. Mark Twain used the club as a sounding board for his own theories: on women suffrage which he first opposed but later accepted enthusiastically; on universal suffrage, which he accepted too after toying with the idea that intellectuals should have more votes than common people.

Inevitably they had a stream of houseguests. Literary people, editors, publishers, newspapermen, used Nook Farm as a half-way stop between Boston and New York. Scores of celebrities came at one time or another, Sarah Orne Jewett of Maine, Joel Chandler Harris, creator of the Uncle Remus stories, Thomas Bailey Aldrich, author of *Story of a Bad*

Boy, William Dean Howells, editor of the *Atlantic Monthly* and always one of Mark Twain's most devoted admirers; the list could go on.

Bret Harte, who had become famous in his own right, more for some verses called the *Heathen Chinee* than for his excellent "The Luck of Roaring Camp," came and stayed for long intervals. He and Mark Twain collaborated on a play called *Ah Sin*, about the shrewd Chinese laundryman of those verses; it was not a success. His visits became more onerous; he borrowed money from Mark, drank up large amounts of his whiskey, complained about the service, and finally said or did something slighting to Livy, for which Mark never forgave him.

Everyone had agreed that Livy was a charming hostess, gracious and thoughtful of the needs of her guests. Yet even with all the servants, she found that looking after the welfare of outsiders left her exhausted. It saddened her too that she had to spend so much time with the guests; she would have liked to have more leisure for her daughters.

Mark, an extrovert, enjoyed the role of host enormously. He liked to have an audience for his stories, to sing from his large repertory, to dance. But even at the moments of his greatest popularity and prosperity, he had a yearning for his "don't-care-a-damn" life in one of those grubby boarding houses of his past, when he had had no money, but no responsibilities either.

The brilliant society into which his marriage to

Livy and his move to Hartford had plunged him did not and could not provide him with the colorful human material which was the source of his best work. For that he had to turn to his past, as a boy and as a young man seeking to find himself. There was too much activity in the present on Farmington Avenue for him to write at the white heat creativity of which he was capable. For that he had to turn to the tranquility of Quarry Farm.

9

quarry farm and the octagonal study

So I knocked off and went to playing billiards for a change.

—Mark Twain

Quarry Farm was a large rambling building with a wide veranda, built on a hill overlooking Elmira and the Chemung River. Originally, the house with seven acres had belonged to Jervis Langdon. He had deeded it to Livy's older sister Susan and her husband Theodore Crane. They had bought more acreage, turned it into a year-round home, and employed a black farmer named Lewis to look after the cattle and hay fields.

Mark and Livy spent their first summer as guests of the Cranes in 1871, just before they moved to Nook Farm. Under her sister's care, Livy was recovering from the long illness that had plagued her in Buffalo. Mark did the major part of the writing on *Roughing It* that summer. The writing was proceeding splendidly; he was turning out thirty or more pages a day. Joe Goodman, who had been his editor at the Virginia City *Enterprise*, paid a visit, read the manuscript, and encouraged him to continue.

Of all the well-meaning editor friends Mark Twain had known over the years, Goodman was the one with the soundest judgment. He never urged Mark to tone down his writing or make it more refined, as some others did, including his beloved wife Livy. Nor was he as lavish with his praise as William Dean Howells, who for years served as Mark Twain's literary mentor. Above all he, urged Mark to be himself at all times and write about the things he knew best. He preferred *Roughing It* to *Innocents* and history has born him out. Today *Innocents*, with all its amusing touches and excellent reporting, seems dated; its youthful prejudices irritate. *Roughing It* remains as vivid a picture of the early West as has ever been written.

The Clemens family were back at Quarry Farm in June 1874, with the new baby, Clara, and two-year-old Susy in tow. Susan Crane had prepared a delightful surprise for her brother-in-law. This was a one-room study, shaped like a Mississippi River pilot house, complete with a fireplace, built about a hundred yards from the main house. Mark was delighted:

> It is the loveliest study you ever saw . . .
> octagonal with a peaked roof, each face filled
> with a spacious window, and it sits perched
> in complete isolation on the very top of an
> elevation that commands leagues of valley and
> city and retreating ranges of distant blue hills.
> It is a cozy nest . . . and when the storms sweep
> down the remote valley and the lightning flashes
> behind the hills beyond and the rain beats upon
> the roof over my head, imagine the luxury of it.

In truth he seemed more elated about this tiny study than about his immensely expensive house on Farmington Avenue, which was now nearly ready for his occupancy. He furnished the study with a round writing table, two chairs, a sofa, and later with a typewriter. Each morning after his favorite breakfast of steak and coffee, he climbed up to it and wrote until dinnertime, without even stopping for lunch. Finished pages piled up on the floor to be assembled later. On hot days he opened the windows wide—and had to anchor his papers "with brickbats." He worked like that summer after summer.

No one can say whether Mark Twain would have been as productive and creative without his study, but Susan Crane still deserves a vote of thanks from all his admirers for providing an ambiance in which he could work at his best.

One project of that summer of 1874 was a play about Colonel Sellers, who first appeared in *The Gilded Age*. With John T. Raymond in the title role, the play made Mark Twain a lot of money and was in fact one of the most popular and profitable plays of the 1870s. He was always interested in the theater, tried doing plays or dramatizing his own works again and again, but nothing else was as successful as the Colonel Sellers play.

Another summer project was "A True Story," a tale about an elderly black woman who was separated from her son at a slave auction and was not reunited with him until twenty-two years later during the Civil War. This was his first piece published in the highbrow *Atlantic Monthly*. They paid him two cents a word, more than they had ever given a writer before. Some readers were stunned to find nothing funny in the story; they kept looking for the catch.

That summer he was also toying with the idea of writing a story set in Hannibal. It shaped up gradually as a tale about a boy named Tom Sawyer. He improvised as he went along without an overall plan, so that every so often he found himself at a dead end, having no idea what would happen next. He was just as uncertain as to whether he was writing it for boys or adults. By September he had written about 400 pages and had come to a dead halt.

So he knocked off, as he wrote a friend, and went out to play a game of billiards. "When the tank runs dry you've only to leave it alone and it will fill up again in time."

Over the winter the tank filled up. By November 1875, he had turned over the manuscript of *The Adventures of Tom Sawyer* to Bliss, who did not publish it until the fall of 1876. Although William Dean Howells heralded it as "altogether the best boy's story I ever read," sales for the first year were a mere 24,000—compared to 27,000 for a far less important book of Mark Twain's published the year before, *Sketches, New and Old*. *Tom Sawyer* missed out on the prepublication publicity Bliss usually gave his books, for which Mark Twain could not forgive him.

The summer of 1876, Mark Twain worked on a sequel to Tom Sawyer in his Quarry Farm studio, calling it *Huckleberry Finn*. It did not occur to him that *Huck* would be acclaimed his greatest book. He liked it only tolerably well, he said, and might well burn the manuscript. It would not be finished until seven years later.

The Prince and the Pauper, A Tramp Abroad, Life on the Mississippi, and *A Yankee in King Arthur's Court* were all written in that octagonal study between the years 1877 and 1888. The last thing he wrote there was a story called "A Dog's Tale," done in 1903. The study has now been transferred to the Elmira College campus. Furnished as Mark Twain had it, it is a place of pilgrimage. Only the view over the hills is missing.

For Mark Twain, Quarry Farm was a retreat from the world. For his three daughters, Susy and Clara and Jean, the youngest, born in July of 1880, it was a summer playground. They adored running up and down its green slopes, riding on top of a hay wagon, or taking their cats out for a walk.

Mark Twain loved cats himself. They had a large population of them: Fraulein, Blatherskite, Sour Mash, Stray Kit, Sin, Satan. When one of them died, there was an elaborate funeral. At bedtime, the girls would beg their father for a cat story. One of them, published posthumously as "A Cat-Tale," was about "a noble big cat, whose Christian name was Catasauqua." Catasauqua had a family of catlings, among them Cattaraugus, who had "high impulses and a pure heart," and Catiline, who had a self-seeking nature, whose motives were nearly always base, and who was "insincere, vain and foolish."

Little Jean had a donkey named Kiditchin. Her father made up a poem about her, which began:

> In summer days Kiditchin
> Thou'rt dear from nose to britchin
> Waw .... he!

Mark Twain once mounted Kiditchin to show his children how to ride her, but she flung him off. He said it was because she had read his poem.

It was not always easy to be the daughters of the famous Mark Twain, but there were compensations.

Of the three of them, Susy, the oldest, was his favorite. She was the most imaginative, the most sensitive, the most thoughtful. Jean liked cows better than books. Clara was the musician. When Mark Twain was fifty and Susy was fourteen, she started writing his biography:

"We are a very happy family," she wrote. "We consist of Papa, Mama, Jean, Clara and me. It is papa I am writing about, and I shall have no trouble in not knowing what to say about him, as he is a *very* striking character." She described him as having "beautiful gray hair," a Roman nose "which greatly improves the beauty of his features," kind blue eyes and a small mustache. All his features were perfect "exept [sic] that he hasn't extraordinary teeth." It was true he had a temper—"but we all of us have in this family."

In one part of her biography, Susy describes how she and Clara looked over her mother's shoulder as she was going over the manuscript of *Huckleberry Finn* to decide what parts she must "expergate." (All their married life, Mark Twain let Livy edit his books, taking out anything she did not consider to be in good taste. Indeed he sometimes boasted that he put in improper things just to give her something to remove.)

"I remember one part perticuklarly," wrote Susy, "which was perfectly fascinating it was so terrible

. . . and oh, with what despair, we saw mama turn down the leaf on which it was written."

In 1889, a young British journalist, born in Bombay, was in America writing articles for an Indian paper. His name was Rudyard Kipling. Kipling decided to track down the man he had learned to love and admire, "the great and godlike Clemens," as he called the author of *Tom Sawyer*. Kipling first went to Buffalo, and was sent to Hartford, where he was told that Mark Twain might be in Europe, but that he might also be in Elmira. He was in Elmira next morning, calling it a town "desolated by railway tracks," with suburbs given up to "the manufacture of door-sashes and window-frames, and where the Chemung River flowed "generally up and down the town, and had just finished flooding a few of the main streets."

No one seemed to know where "the man Clemens" lived. Finally a policeman said he had seen Twain, or someone like him, driving in a buggy the day before, and directed the stranger to Quarry Farm. He hired a hack to take him up the "awful hill" to the farm only to hear that Mark Twain had walked downtown to see his brother-in-law. At Charles Langdon's house, Kipling finally caught up with him.

They talked about a wide range of things, about Sir Walter Scott, whom Mark Twain considered a slovenly writer, and about Congress, whose members were so frequently governed by self-interest. Mark

87

Twain waxed eloquent on his pet subject of the shortcomings of the copyright system for writers, and pirate publishers who printed books and paid the authors nothing.

In a story in the New York *Herald,* Kipling boasted that while some people thought themselves privileged to walk arm in arm with a Viceroy, *he* had seen *Mark Twain* one golden morning, shaken his hand, smoked two cigars with him, and talked with him for more than two hours.

Mark Twain was almost equally impressed with his young visitor. Afterward he said that Kipling knew everything there was to know and that he, Twain, knew the rest.

10

america's roving ambassador

A man with a hump-backed uncle mustn't make fun
of another man's cross-eyed aunt.

—Mark Twain

In addition to the two quite separate lives he lived
at Nook Farm and Quarry Farm, Mark Twain had a
third life, that of foreign traveler, which ran con-
comitantly with the other two. It is estimated that
this most American of writers spent an estimated
one-sixth of his life abroad. He always said he hated

to travel but he continued to do it almost to the day of his death.

In 1872 he set out for London to talk to his British publisher, Routledge and Sons, who had published *The Innocents Abroad* and were planning their edition of *Roughing It*. He also wanted to protest a pirated edition of *The Celebrated Jumping Frog of Calaveras*, which an unscrupulous publisher (not Routledge) had extended to include works not by Mark Twain at all. Ironically, the *Jumping Frog*, even more than *Innocents*, had spread his name in England.

It was his first long separation from Livy since their marriage and he missed her. Off the coast of Ireland, on the way to Liverpool, he wrote: "I am standing high on the stern of the ship, looking westward, with my hands to my mouth trumpet fashion, yelling across the tossing waste of waves, 'I LOVE YOU, LIVY DARLING ! ! ! ' "

In London, his Routledge and Sons editors took him to lunch. That evening he was invited to the Savage Club, where he met the actor, Henry Irving, and Henry Stanley, the man who had "discovered" the missionary David Livingston in darkest Africa. In the next days he was invited to the Lord Mayor's dinner, to the Guildhall Dinner of the Sheriffs of London, and to many private London homes and country estates. He was introduced daily to celebrities who wanted to meet him, novelists Charles Reade and Charles Kingsley, Robert Browning, the poet, various ambassadors, statesmen, and members of British nobility. Though it was still early in his career, he was treated like a celebrity himself.

This initial welcome was heady as wine, all the more so because in the United States Mark Twain was still being snubbed as a mere humorist by the New England intelligentsia. He returned home for Christmas, but was back in May 1873, with Livy and little Susy, to bring Routledge the recently completed manuscript of *The Gilded Age*. His welcome in London was as warm as before. Important personages came in droves to the Langham Hotel where the Clemens family was staying. They were invited to a string of luncheons and dinners held in the honor of Mark Twain.

En route for a vacation in Scotland, Mark and Livy stopped in historic York, where in addition to half-timbered Tudor houses from the era of Queen Elizabeth, they found ancient ruins dating back to the days of Danish dominion and "melancholy old stone coffins" which may have been placed there by Roman soldiers before the Christian era. Mark Twain's fascination with early English history began there.

They visited Ireland and France too but were back in London in October, where Mark Twain was scheduled for a week's lecture engagement on "Our Fellow Savages of the Sandwich Islands." People came the first night perhaps from curiosity. For the rest of the week, the hall was sold out; the staid

Britishers showered him with applause and laughter.

He returned for another lecture week in December, this time on "Roughing It on the Silver Frontier," which proved no less popular. Mark Twain was used to crowded halls back home, but not to such an aristocratic audience, which arrived in fine coaches and dressed as for a ball.

In the end he had to hire a secretary to answer invitations to suppers, drives, weekends, croquet, garden parties, and the like. Most gratifying of all was a short note from Lord Alfred Tennyson, thanking him for some complimentary tickets. Hardly anybody could get a Tennyson autograph at that time. In later years, the poet would comment about Mark Twain's "finesse in his choice of words, his feeling for . . . the precise shade of meaning desired." He was astute enough to recognize what many others did not, that Mark Twain was a superb craftsman, fully cognizant of the wide gap between the right word and the word that was almost right.

The cliché that the British have no sense of humor proved a myth. They could even laugh at themselves. Mark Twain risked a letter to the London *Morning Post*, in December 1873, in which he said that since no notable government figures attended his lectures he had contracted with a waxworks man for "a couple of kings and some nobility." But the porter had fallen and smashed Henry VIII, he continued, then something let go in William the Conqueror and all the sawdust fell out. . . .

If any Britisher took offense at such levity, he never heard of it.

Under all that adulation, Mark Twain became an ardent Anglophile, and for a time held the view that the British system of government was far superior to the American system—less corrupt for one thing. His love affair with England at white heat temperatures lasted through the 1870s.

The contrast between his stature in Europe and America was brought home to him in 1877. He had been asked to speak in Boston, at a dinner in honor of the seventieth birthday of John Greenleaf Whittier. Oliver Wendell Holmes, Ralph Waldo Emerson, Henry Wadsworth Longfellow were in the audience. Mark Twain in his speech offered them a bit of fantasy he had unwittingly concocted.

In the Sierra foothills one day, he said, he had stopped in a miner's cabin and identified himself. The miner told him that he had been visited by three other literary men the night before. They had gorged themselves on beans and whiskey and left in the morning with the miner's only pair of shoes. They had said their names were Emerson, Holmes, and Longfellow. Indignantly, Mark had assured him that the three were imposters, they could not possibly be the gentlemen to whom the world "played loving reverence."

At that, the miner looked him up and down coldly, and demanded: "Ah, imposters were they? And you?"

Mark Twain, who usually knew his audiences, expected the last line to bring down the house. Instead, he was greeted with dead silence. Even his good friend, William Dean Howells, looked horrified. For reasons that are still not very clear, the audience decided that the outlaw from Missouri had made an unforgettable and unforgivable gaffe.

No one felt worse about the affair than Mark Twain himself. Convinced of his guilt at last, he wrote humble apologies to Longfellow, Holmes, and Emerson. The first two wrote back cheerily that they had not minded. Emerson, who was very old and somewhat senile, had not understood what had been said. Thus it was Boston society that was offended, and not the writers. A long time later Mark Twain reread his speech and decided it was rather amusing after all. At the time he wanted only to get away and "breathe the free air of Europe and lay in a stock of self-respect and independence."

They sailed for Germany in April 1878—Mark, Livy, her friend, Miss Spaulding, Susy, Clara, and the nursemaid Rosa. (This was before the birth of Jean, their youngest girl.) In Heidelberg they settled down in a spacious apartment, with a view of Heidelberg Castle and the "haze-empurpled valley of the Rhine." The whole family wrestled with German, "an awful language." Mark jotted down in his notebook a dream that all bad foreigners went to a German heaven, where they had such trouble making themselves understood that they wished they had gone to "the other place."

On August 1, the Reverend Joseph Twichell joined them and he and Mark set out on a leisurely walking tour through the Black Forest. The minister later said that his companion felt it discourteous to pass another hiker, and that he was timid about asking questions of strangers, and that he could not bear to see a horse whipped. During their walk, Mark confessed that he did not believe that the Bible was inspired by God. His confession did not alter their friendship. Their hike ended in Switzerland, where Livy and the little girls were waiting. Twichell left for home but the Clemens family went on a tour of Venice, Florence, and Rome, during which they bought paintings, marble statuary and a massive carved bed with serpentine columns decorated by cupids for their Nook Farm home.

They spent the winter in Munich. Mark Twain rented a room apart from the family to work on *A Tramp Abroad,* a travel book about his hike with Joe Twichell. The writing went slowly; he was never much interested in this book.

In late February they went to Paris. The weather was cold and wet and foggy. Mark Twain, who had so enjoyed Paris on his first visit, turned against France and the French, a prejudice he never really dissolved. "France has neither winter, nor summer, nor morals," he wrote. He said that the Reign of Terror, which followed in the wake of the French Revolution, showed that the people were all savages —dukes, lawyers, blacksmiths alike. He spared no sympathy for Marie Antoinette but adored Napoleon, and became absorbed with the idea of writing a book about Joan of Arc. Livy and the children studied French.

Within ten years Mark Twain had acquired a different perspective on the Reign of Terror. There were in fact two Reigns of Terror, he wrote in *A Connecticut Yankee in King Arthur's Court*, published in 1889. The one before the "blessed" French Revolution lasted a thousand years and inflicted death upon a hundred million. The "minor" Reign of Terror after the Revolution lasted a mere few months and at most resulted in 10,000 deaths. One of Mark Twain's virtues was that he was not abashed at discarding opinions he had outgrown.

They were back in New York by September 1879. The voyage set a pattern that Mark Twain followed the rest of his life.

Their longest stay abroad began in 1891. One reason for their departure was lower living costs. Though they always lived extravagantly in Europe, it was still much cheaper than living extravagantly at home. To save money they had closed up the Nook Farm in Hartford temporarily; they would never live there again. Europe was their home for much of the next nine years. They wandered through Sweden, Switzerland, France, Germany, Italy, Austria, and always back to England, where Mark Twain's fame and popularity grew beyond measure. London stopped traffic for him. *Punch* featured him in numerous cartoons. The Russian novelist Turgenev, an exile in London, sought him out. His list of ever-expanding friends included Anthony Trollope, Wilkie Collins, Lewis Carroll of *Alice in Wonderland* fame, George Bernard Shaw, practically everybody who had done something important.

On the continent the highest European royalty paid him tribute. Queen Elizabeth of Rumania, a writer herself, told him she owed him the intensest of all joys—hero-worship—and "days and days" of forgetfulness from troubles. In 1892 he was guest of honor of Kaiser William II, who said that *Life on the Mississippi* was his greatest book. He met Emperor Francis Joseph of Austria in 1899, and found him full of "plain, good, attractive human nature." At least, he added, tongue in cheek as usual, he must have those qualities to unbend to him; he could not unbend if he were the emperor.

He enjoyed such encounters mightily but was not awed by them. In "Extract from Captain Stormfield's Visit to Heaven," written in his old age, kings were reduced to ordinary people: Charles II had become a comedian; Richard the Lionhearted was a boxer; Henry VIII was a tragedian, playing all the scenes in which he had killed people.

11

a writer turns publisher

The critic assumes every time that if a book doesn't meet
the cultivated-class standard, it isn't valuable . . . I have
never tried in even one single little instance to help cul-
tivate the cultivated classes.

—Mark Twain in a letter to Andrew Lang

A Tramp Abroad, based on the hike through the
Black Forest that Mark Twain had taken with Reverend Twichell, was published by Elisha Bliss in
1879. It was the last book Mark submitted to him. He
had found out that his books were making enormous

profits for the American Publishing Company, of which he received, comparatively, a pittance. He demanded half the profits for *Tramp*, which Bliss promised him but which Twain never got. Mark Twain walked out on him.

His next three books were published by James R. Osgood of Boston: *The Stolen White Elephant*, a collection of sketches; *The Prince and The Pauper*, in 1880; and *Old Times on the Mississippi* (later retitled *Life on the Mississippi*) in 1883. Mark Twain, accustomed to huge sales, was disappointed. He liked Osgood personally but it was obvious that he knew little about the sales campaign needed for subscription publishing.

Life on the Mississippi, the second of his books that Osgood published, was pure Americana. This was the record of an era and a profession as only Mark Twain could have told it. It is generally held to be his greatest nonfiction book.

The Prince and the Pauper, set in England in the time of Edward VI, was a fantasy about a king's son and a poor lad who changed places with each other. It brought Mark Twain a type of praise he had never had before. Eastern reviewers used such adjectives as refined, pure, and ennobling. Harriet Beecher Stowe told him it was the best book for young people ever written. For Livy it was the sort of book she had always wished he would write and known he could write. Even the English reviews of *The Prince and the Pauper* were complimentary.

Only Joe Goodman of Virginia City took a sour view. Why did he have to go "groping among the driftwood of the Deluge for a topic?" he grumbled to his old friend and protégé. Goodman was at this time on the verge of making his own reputation, for his researches in the Yucatan and his initial work toward deciphering the Mayan language.

In spite of Mark Twain's complaints about his publisher, *The Prince and the Pauper* rapidly gained popularity. It is unique among his works of fiction in that its structure, as a novel, is flawless. Mark Twain always had trouble with plots and usually left loose ends hanging. Since these "loose ends" were invariably amusing, most people have never minded.

In 1884, Mark Twain started his own publishing business, and set his nephew, Charles Webster, husband of Pamela's daughter, Annie, in official charge. Charlie had previously worked for "Uncle Sam" as a sort of combination errand boy, secretary, and lawyer. His new role, as head of Charles L. Webster and Company, was to prove no less harassing.

The first book the new company issued was *The Adventures of Huckleberry Finn,* published some eight years after Mark Twain commenced work on it. It received the coldest reception of any of his books. Literary magazines ignored it. The comic magazine *Life* called it "coarse and dreary fun." A month after it came out, the Library Committee of Concord, Massachusetts, banned it on the grounds that it was "rough, coarse, and inelegant." Concord resident Louisa May Alcott, author of *Little Women*, said acidly that if Mr. Clemens could not think of anything better to tell "our pure-minded lads and lasses," he had better stop writing for them.

The Concord attack roused Mark Twain from his depression about the book's fate. He wrote Webster that being banned in Concord, was "a rattling tip-top puff," and was sure to sell 25,000 copies. He was right. Within a year *Huck* sold 42,000 copies, more than *Innocents*, his previous bestseller. It would, in time, sell more than ten million copies and be translated all over the world. It would be called the greatest work of American literature and a world classic.

Tom Sawyer had appealed because boys identified with Tom and imagined themselves having the same adventures, and because grown men saw in Tom their own youthful rebellion against authority. Huck, the ragged, illiterate son of a worthless drunkard, was a more universal figure. In his struggle to be himself and to survive, one senses the struggle of the whole of humanity. When Huck decides he would, literally, rather go to hell than turn in "Nigger Jim," his companion on the raft, as a runaway slave, he lends nobility to the entire human race.

Literary critic Maxwell Geismar speaks of "a Twainian dimension of comedy and tragedy alike" which makes Mark Twain "unique in letters." In *Huckleberry Finn*, Mark Twain, the humorist, the comedian, the man who could make anyone and everyone laugh, is just beginning his probe into the darker, irrefutably tragic, side of life.

Huck Finn's immortal fame did not come at once. In spite of its substantial sales, the Webster company could not survive on this one book. Later in 1884, when Mark Twain was in New York to give a lecture, he heard that General Grant had decided to write his memoirs. To get the Grant memoirs was the biggest scoop in publishing and one that Mark did not want to miss.

As a promising young author, he had been presented to President Grant in the White House in the 1870s. Grant was not a talkative man. After the exchange of courtesies, there was dead silence. Mark Twain burst out: "Mr. President, I seem to be a little embarrassed. Are you?" His sally produced a grim smile.

They met again in November 1879 in Chicago, where Grant was the guest of honor at a Civil War veterans' reunion, and where Mark had been invited to speak at the Palmer House banquet that climaxed the celebration. He was the fifteenth speaker and was not called on until two in the morning, at which point the 500 veterans were surfeited with oysters, champagne, and rum punch.

He made his toast, not "to the women," as was customary, but "to the babies—as they comfort us in our sorrows, let us not forget them in our festivities." He reminded this gathering of men-of-war that they might be majestic on the battlefield but that when their own infants pulled their whiskers and twisted their noses they had to take it. He pointed out that all of them had once been babies—that even their former commander-in-chief had once been lying in a cradle "trying to find some way of getting his big toe in his mouth."

Once again he was risking the fiasco of his Holmes-Longfellow-Emerson speech, but he got out of it with a clever phrase, and then everyone was laughing—even the iron man, General Grant.

They had become friends. In the intervening years Mark had visited him often, listened to his reminiscences, urged him repeatedly to write his memoirs. Grant was rich and not ambitious; he never bothered. But by 1884, his entire fortune had vanished through some unfortunate business deals and the betrayal of a man he had trusted. The memoirs had become a necessity if his family was not to go hungry.

Mark Twain, on hearing the rumors, promptly called on Grant at his home on 60th Street, talking to him of the advantages of subscription publishing and of putting his memoirs with the Charles L. Webster Company. Grant said that Century had already offered him a 10 percent royalty. Mark Twain countered with an offer of a 20 percent royalty and a $10,000 advance, or 70 percent of the publisher's profits, if he preferred. In the end Grant, somewhat overwhelmed, agreed to the latter offer.

Even then, though no one knew it, he was a condemned man dying of cancer. By sheer will power, he worked through pain and exhaustion, writing as much as 9,000 words at a time. When writing became too difficult, he dictated to a stenographer. Three days after the manuscript was completed, he was dead.

Sales exceeded even Mark Twain's most optimistic predictions. The first royalty check Webster paid Grant's widow was for $200,000, the largest ever paid an author in publishing history. In all, the memoirs earned the Grant family half a million dollars.

Hoping to duplicate the Grant success, Webster and Twain published a life of Pope Leo XIII, in six languages simultaneously, but the sales were mediocre. They issued memoirs by Sheridan, Sherman, and other generals; none of them could rival Grant's clear and terse writing.

Webster fell seriously ill in the late 1880s; his editorship was taken over by the young business manager, Frederick J. Hall. In 1889, when Hall was working on the manuscript of *A Connecticut Yankee in King Arthur's Court,* he wrote Mark that the printer's proofreader was improving his punctuation. Mark Twain, who took pride in both his spelling and his punctuation, claimed that he telegraphed orders to have the proofreader shot without giving him time to pray.

Connecticut Yankee, published in 1889, was begun as a burlesque on knights in shining armor, who had no way of blowing their noses or scratching a fly. It developed as an attack on the evils of feudalism, monarchy, and the power of the church in the time of King Arthur. Perhaps unintentionally, the book also satirizes modern industrial civilization. Yankee Hank Morgan, transported from Connecticut, is horrified at the backwardness, cruelty, and poverty of the feudal world, and sets out to build a democracy by introducing an industrial culture. The results are more burlesque: knights riding bicycles, knights carrying picket signs advertising brandname toothpaste. More hilarious is a scene in which Hank attempts to find suitable quarters for a herd of pigs which he has been informed are bewitched duchesses.

Not surprisingly, the book offended many Britishers. The few journals that mentioned it at all condemned it as dull and in bad taste. The *Spectator* wrote that the author had "surpassed himself as a low comedian in literature by the manner in which he has vaulted into the charmed circle of Arthurian romance." The general verdict was that Mark Twain had overstepped himself, not for mocking the institution of monarchy, which the English could have taken in their stride, but for making a travesty of the lovely legends of King Arthur and his Round Table. Rudyard Kipling, desolate, refused to belief that his idol and hero could have written such a lame book.

Americans liked it. Reviewers for the most part

ignored the social aspects of the books and talked about its humor. It would be a successful motion picture and is a television favorite.

The Webster company published one more Mark Twain novel, *The American Claimant*, a variation of the Colonel Sellers story, which, like all of his works categorized as "minor," had some very clever parts. They issued *The Library of Humor*, an anthology of American humorists compiled by Mark Twain and William Dean Howells. Charles Webster died in 1891. The business manager, Frederick Hall, struggled valiantly to keep the firm going, but it was obviously in heavy financial trouble.

12

the paige typesetter and other follies

Every man is a moon and has a dark side which he never shows to anybody.

—Mark Twain

In the early 1870s, Mark Twain patented a scrapbook of his own invention. It had gummed pages which had only to be moistened for the "scraps" to adhere to them. His *Quaker City* friend, Dan Slote, manufactured "Mark Twain's Self-Pasting Scrapbook." Both made money from it. All his adult life Mark was interested in inventions of all sorts, his own and other people's, but the scrapbook was the only one that paid for itself.

He applied for a patent on "Improvement in Adjustable and Detachable Straps for Garments." He considered a concoction of kerosene and cheap perfume to cure chilblains. He proposed a railroad steam brake only to be told that Westinghouse had discarded the same idea. He worked on a paddle wheel suitable for icy waters, a way of casting brass dies to stamp book covers and wallpaper, developed a "perpetual calendar," shared an interest in a patented bed clamp to keep children from kicking off their blankets at night.

In his preoccupation, he was not alone. As the industrial age became full blown, people all over the country were devoting time, energy, and money to discover some household labor-saving device or mechanical gadget or revolutionary process that would net them a fortune. Mark Twain's brother Orion, was always working on something or other, including a flying machine. The number was legion of men convinced they had a clue to a perpetual motion machine. For all the failures or minor successes, there was the shining example of the few who had transformed the world—Thomas Edison, Alexander Bell, Nikola Tesla.

Mark Twain was a pioneer in welcoming the new inventions. He owned the first private telephone in Hartford. He bought a typewriter; *Tom Sawyer* may have been the first book manuscript to be typed. He dictated part of another book into a phonograph. He adopted the first fountain pens. Long before the word "robot" was in common usage, he was humanizing machines in his mind. To Livy he extolled the talents of a "charming machine" that made, gummed, printed, counted, and packaged 9,000 envelopes an hour. He invested more money than he usually cared to admit on various contraptions that caught his fancy.

In 1880, a Hartford jeweler with whom Mark Twain was playing billiards told him about a typesetting machine which a man named James Paige was developing at the Colt arms factory. To Mark Twain, who had passed so many tedious hours setting type by hand in his youth, it sounded like a stunning idea. When he saw the typesetter at the Colt factory he was much impressed. In the flush of his enthusiasm, he called it a magnificent creature ranking only second to man. Very promptly he invested $5,000 to perfect it.

James Paige had received the patent for his typesetter in 1874 in Rochester. He then moved to Hartford, where investment capital and skilled mechanics were readily available. He had a likable personality, dressed well, and had a gift of persuasion second to none. Ten years later Mark Twain could still speak of him as a poet "whose sublime creations are written in steel." By that time Mark Twain was putting some

$4,000 a month in the typesetter, money that Livy had inherited, money that should have gone back into the Webster Publishing Company.

The Paige Typesetter had 18,000 separate parts. Just when everything seemed under control, something would break down. On occasion Mark Twain brought possible investors to see it only to find that Paige had taken it all apart. The truth was that the typesetter was too delicate and too complicated for practical use. Mark Twain refused to lose faith, sustained by his dream that the typesetter would make him a millionaire many times over. Only his own Colonel Sellers could have held on so long to such a foolish dream.

In his obsession he ignored other similar inventions. The idea was not new. As far back as 1842, a machine designed by Henry Bessemer was setting type commercially. Ottmar Mergenthaler patented his linotype in Baltimore in 1885; a year later the New York *Tribune* had put it into operation.

His typesetter, Mark Twain pointed out, did not get drunk and never joined the union. He did not give up even after he had fed it $300,000. It was in the midst of this imbroglio of debts and disaster that in 1891 he and Livy closed up the Hartford house for their long stay in Europe, where, they reasoned, they could live so much more economically.

On one of several trips back to the States which

Mark Twain made to survey his tattered fortunes, he met a wealthy Standard Oil executive, Henry H. Rogers, who had long been a staunch admirer. Rogers was ruthless in business. For Mark Twain, he proved a friend in need, a man of infinite tact and understanding. One night after they had been playing billiards together, Mark told him the whole painful story of his tangled finances.

Rogers volunteered to take over, saying it was no burden but a pleasure to help a friend. He loaned him enough money to keep Webster Publishing Company going a little longer. He gave his time and his experience and asked for nothing in return. Mark wrote him gratefully that in all his fifty-nine years he had never before found a friend who would put out a hand to pull him ashore when he was in deep water. The combination of Mark Twain, the rebel, and Henry Rogers, the robber baron, has struck some people as odd, and Mark Twain has since been accused of selling out to big business. It was not true. He never criticized Rogers personally, but in the years to come he would become increasingly vocal about the crimes of money-mad industrialists.

Rogers decreed the Paige typesetter a failure and advised Mark to forget about it. He docilely agreed. On Roger's proposal, the Webster Publishing Company declared bankruptcy in April 1894, three years after the death of Charlie Webster. The Hartford *Courant* headlined the story as "Mark Twain's Failure." The firm owed Mark Twain about $60,000 borrowed money, owed Livy $65,000, and owed 96 creditors an average of about $1,000 each.

Livy, who recoiled at the shame of debts, proposed giving the creditors the Hartford house, which was in her name, as well as the rights to Mark Twain's books. Henry Rogers, now in control, said firmly that this was not the way to handle the matter. Mark Twain's books belonged to him and no one else. Instead of letting Livy sell their home, he put her on the list as a "preferred creditor" of the publishing firm. Yet he sided with her that all creditors should be paid in full. An ordinary businessman could get away with paying creditors 33 percent on the dollar, but "a literary man's reputation is his life."

With all his worries and all his traipsing back and forth across the Atlantic, Mark Twain had kept on writing. *The Tragedy of Pudd'nhead Wilson*, his third novel set in the Mississippi Valley, and one of his most important, was published in 1894. The scene is another "drowsing" river town—Dawson's Landing. Wilson, a lawyer, is an intelligent, decent man, but when he arrives he makes the mistake of saying something witty which no one understands, and so is dubbed "Pudd'nhead." From that point on he never has a client (as had happened to Mark's father, and was still happening to Orion). It is not Pudd'nhead but Roxanna, a mulatto slave, who is the story's protagonist.

Roxanna is a beautiful woman who could easily

have passed for white if everyone in town had not known she was one-sixteenth black. She has a baby son whom she names Valet de Chambre (later shortened to Chambers). He has blue eyes and flaxen hair and looks exactly like little Tom, the son of Roxy's master, Percy Driscoll. When Driscoll threatens to sell his slaves down river for some petty pilfering, Roxanna, terrified, switches the two babies, thinking to save her son from a dreadful fate.

Only Pudd'nhead, who does fingerprinting as a hobby and has taken the fingerprints of the two babies, holds the key to their true identity. The Driscoll boy, as Chambers, becomes a servile nonentity. Roxanna's son, as Tom Driscoll, grows up arrogant, snobbish, and unscrupulous, nor does his conduct change, when Roxanna, in desperation, tells him his true identity. Thus, very subtly, Mark Twain demolishes the doctrine of white supremacy.

The plot has several ramifications. There is a subplot involving some handsome Italian twins who come to stay in Dawson's Landing. Through it all, the character of Roxanna dominates the story. Up to this time American writers had nearly always treated women slaves as stereotypes. Roxanna evolves as a complex personality, sometimes full of laughter and sometimes bitter, at once fearful and courageous, warmhearted and capable of immense self-sacrifice, but strong and unyielding.

Also in 1894, *Tom Sawyer Abroad* was published simultaneously in New York and London. This is a delightful science fiction story for boys—more fiction than science to be sure. Narrated by Huck Finn, it tells of a trip in a balloon with Tom and Jim and the balloon's mad professor inventor who, fortunately, falls out of it on their first day up. The balloon, which they can propel up and down and forward and backward at will, takes them to the Sahara, where they are involved in some splendid adventures with Arab caravans, dervishes, lions, and the like.

In January 1895, he finished another short novel, *Tom Sawyer, Detective,* in which Tom successfully plays the role of a Sherlock Holmes. The story, which has an abundance of corpses in the best murder mystery tradition, was based on an actual Swedish criminal trial.

Mark Twain's interest in detective writing was not new. Off and on over the years he had experimented with this intriguing technique. He approached success only when he took to burlesquing the formula detective story. For this purpose he created an amateur detective named Simon Wheeler whose antics he recounted in several sketches, an unfinished novel, and an unproduced play.

Also early in 1895, he finished his full-length book, *The Personal Recollection of Joan of Arc,* which he considered a labor of love. When it was published the following year, people were astounded that a reprobate like Mark Twain could produce such a saintly book.

None of these literary efforts was sufficient to cope

'with the great mountain of his debts. In the spring of 1895, when the bankruptcy proceedings were all in order, he declared that he would now "cease from idling" and go back to work. By work, he meant giving lectures, a sure source of income whenever he needed ready cash. Only this time he would have to do it in a big way; he would take a lecture tour around the world, traveling westward. Major James Pond, Redpath's successor, as his lecture agent, started writing letters and got him signed up for twelve months in advance.

Livy and the girls were taking a vacation at lovely Quarry Farm, a welcome break in their European exile. Mark could not bear to leave them all for such a long stretch. In the end they compromised. Livy and Clara would go with him, but they would leave Susy and little Jean behind in the care of Mrs. Crane, their aunt. As their train pulled out of Elmira, on July 14, 1895, Susy stood on the platform and waved to Clara and her parents.

Major Pond and his wife escorted them as they crossed the American continent in a blare of publicity. They stopped for speech-making in Cleveland, Duluth, Minneapolis, St. Paul, Winnipeg, five towns in Montana, and six in Oregon and Washington. Never had he been received so warmly in his own country. Local celebrities and old acquaintances were on hand to welcome them at each stopping point. His financial troubles had made news, as everything about him always did. His effort to pay

115

off his debts, so in the American tradition, human-
ized him. "Mark's All Right," read a Butte, Montana,
headline. The money gathered from his speeches,
and it was considerable, went straight back to Rogers
for his creditors.

At Vancouver, the Clemens family took leave of
Major and Mrs. Pond and set sail for the longest
and most varied trip of their lives.

13

initiation to colonialism

There are many humorous things in the world; among them the white man's notion that he is less savage than the other savages.

—Mark Twain

In his autobiography, Mark Twain described his world tour succinctly: they lectured and robbed and raided for thirteen months. The details of all he saw, felt, learned, experienced, are in the two-volume book published in 1897—*Following the Equator.*

Like his earlier travel books, *Equator* has a plentiful sprinkling of comic stories, long and short anecdotes, descriptive passages often poetic and beautifully written, and all the padding required to make it the proper size to please a subscription audience. It also has a good deal more social commentary than the others.

With the exception of his stay in Hawaii, he had never before visited any "Third World" countries—those parts of the world with nonwhite populations and religious beliefs not based on orthodox Christianity. The major part of the Third World had been taken over by European powers. The pattern had varied little. First came the explorers. Next came the missionaries followed by merchants looking for slaves or gold or whatever the country had to offer. Then came soldiers, allegedly to protect missionaries and merchants from the natives. The final step was annexation—usually with the excuse that the new colonies needed the benefits of white civilization.

Mark Twain had mocked some of those "benefits" decades before in Hawaii. He could not judge what progress had been made since; their ship was not allowed to land because of a cholera epidemic. They sailed on to Australia, which was still a British dependency; it would become a British Commonwealth in 1901.

In his book *Following the Equator*, Mark Twain would express his doubts as to whether the British were worthy of being the guardians of white civilization. The first British settlement in Australia was a penal colony. The British penal system was then atrocious. One could hardly call a nation civilized if it could look on, unmoved, and "see starving or freezing women hanged for stealing twenty-six cents' worth of bacon or rags," or "boys snatched from their mothers, and men from their families, and sent to the other side of the world for long terms of years for similar trifling offenses."

During his Australian stay, he never saw an aborigine, the native inhabitants, but he praised them for their ability to make fire by friction, to stand pain, and to achieve artistry in their bark paintings. They certainly had "a large distribution of acuteness" to be such "unapproachable trackers and boomerangers." It must be "race aversion" that gave them a reputation for low intelligence. They kept their own population down by infanticide. This was unnecessary after the white man came; he was able to reduce their popuation by 80 percent in twenty years.

Some of the settlers were more humane than others. There was the case of a certain Australian squatter. At Christmas time this squatter invited the black natives to his place and treated them with a plum pudding "sweetened with arsenic." The quick death by poison that the squatter provided them with was "loving-kindness" compared to the usual methods of extermination, wrote Twain with bitter irony. It was far more humane, for example, than burning a man at the stake. Or hunting him and his family with dogs and guns for an afternoon's sport, "filling the region with happy laughter over their sprawling and stumbling flight."

In the province of Queensland, planters needed labor for their sugar cane plantations. They "recruited" Kanaka natives from the Pacific islands. The Kanaka was "cheap, very cheap." The planter paid twenty pounds to the recruiter for "catching" him ("to catch a native" was a missionary expression, Mark Twain learned). The Queensland government demanded a fee of five pounds, plus a five pound deposit for the Kanaka's trip home. To the Kanaka himself, the planter paid about twenty-five pounds for three years' wages—some four shillings a week. For the planter, it was an excellent deal.

What puzzled Mark Twain was why the Kanaka should want to be a recruit. Life on his own island was a continuous holiday. If he needed money for anything he could always sell a couple of bags of copra for a few shillings. In Queensland, he had to work eight to twelve hours a day in the canefields. For white people, Queensland was exceedingly healthy, with a death rate of twelve in 1,000 population. In 1893, the official death rate of the Kanakas was 52 per thousand; for new arrivals the rate soared to 180 per thousand.

Deadpan, Mark Twain suggested that maybe the

"recruiting" was not so voluntary as its reputation. Otherwise why were there so many blood-curdling attacks on the recruiters? A planter protested to him that the Kanaka came to work naked but that when he went home he had a watch, collar, cuffs, boots, and an umbrella. He was somebody in his community. Mark Twain had some thoughts of his own about how long it would take before he discarded all that finery and was comfortably naked again.

In the Fiji Islands he was entranced by the wrinkled old women, the "plump and smily" young girls, the tall, straight, comely, and nobly built young matrons, and the majestic young men clothed in dazzling white with bronze legs bare and hair dyed a rich brick red. He heard that these "savage" Fijis believed that flowers after death rise on the winds and float to heaven, there to flourish in immortal beauty. Just sixty years before, these people had been "sunk in darkness." Now, he noted wryly in *Following the Equator*, they had the bicycle.

He was equally ironic in his book about the French way of spreading white civilization in New Caledonia —"a combination of robbery, humiliation and slow, slow murder, through poverty and the white man's whiskey."

The island of Tasmania was another British take-over and "convict dump." The natives had been exiled to other islands or massacred when they resisted. It was a pity; they were a wonderful people and "ought not to have been wasted." They could have been crossed with whites—which would have improved the whites and done the natives no harm. Mark Twain's offhand advocacy of miscegenation was likely intended to shock those Americans who held that "white blood was better than black blood."

In New Zealand he found the same tragic story. He saw a monument to Englishmen killed in the Maori wars, with the inscription that they "fell in defense of law and order against fanaticism and barbarism." Whose law and order? Whose fanaticism and barbarism? In the home of a friend he saw a picture of a Maori chief of the past and found wholly admirable the flowing tattoo designs and the "intellect and masculinity" in his features.

They left the "down under" territory and sailed to Ceylon. Mark Twain wrote poetically about the beautiful dark-skinned women in their loose and flowing and vividly colored garments and the silver anklets and armbands glowing against their dark flesh. He contrasted their attire with the ugly European dress of the little black children at missionary schools.

Next came a stay in India, where he was far kinder to the British rulers than to those in the South Pacific. One theory is that he was under the influence of Rudyard Kipling, who portrayed the British nabobs in India in heroic terms. Mark Twain contended that English rule was far better for the common people than the rule of their own princess, and claimed that when Governor Warren Hastings "saved the Indian Empire for England," it was the best service ever done to the Indian people. He did not mention the Sepoy Rebellion in *Equator* or any other uprising against British rule.

South Africa was next on Mark Twain's lecture schedule. They landed in Durban in the province of Natal, South Africa's most important port after Cape Town. They saw huge black Zulus in full regalia pulling rickshaws for their white overlords. (The Zulus still pull rickshaws, for tourists.) Mark Twain drove inland along roads lined with poinsettias, cactus trees, and arching flamboyant trees, to the beautiful, hilly, and unproductive homeland of the Zulu people—to which he gave the name it still bears—Valley of a Thousand Hills.

"Africa has been as coolly divided up and portioned out among the gang as if they had bought it and paid for it," he wrote about this continent, which was then almost entirely under the rule of England, France, Germany, Spain, Italy, and the Belgian King Leopold II.

The first Europeans in South Africa had been the Dutch, who had settled in Cape Town; their descendants, the Boers, had retreated to the north, leaving the Cape to the English. The English had also driven them out of Natal, whereupon they had trekked to the high veld of central South Africa and established the Orange Free State and the Transvaal. The English let them alone until gold and diamonds were found within their boundaries.

When Mark Twain arrived in Natal, in 1895, people were talking about the raid led by Sir Leander Starr Jameson into Boer territory. Officially the raid was unauthorized but in fact it had the support of Cecil Rhodes, diamond mogul and Prime Minister of Cape Colony. The raid was the prelude to the Boer War which began in 1899, and which the British eventually won.

Mark Twain sided with the Boers in that war, seeing them as the oppressed in an unequal struggle, yet he recognized that the Boers themselves were guilty of heinous crimes against the African peoples. There was a case similar to his Australian squatter with the arsenic; the Boers had forced 500 "kaffirs" —their name for Africans—into a cave and smoked them to death. Heavily sarcastic, Mark Twain praised them for carrying out their mass murder so swiftly.

He had no mercy for the ambitious Cecil Rhodes. "Mr. Rhodes and his gang" he would write in *Equator*, had robbed the Mashonas and Matabeles tribes of part of their lands (in Rhodesia) in the "old style of purchase for a song." Then they forced a quarrel and took the rest of their lands, and seized all their cattle on the pretext that the cattle belonged to their king, not to them; the "gang" had already tricked and assassinated that king. Next they issued regulations that the natives must work for the settlers, thus neglecting their own farms. This was worse slavery than the American kind, Mark Twain believed. When the Rhodesian slave was sick or old, his master had no obligation to support him.

Their South African hosts invited the Clemens family to visit the gold mines of Johannesburg and the diamond mines of Kimberly—where Mark Twain was allowed to participate in the final sorting—and, so he said, drew out a diamond the size of half an almond. They ended up in lovely Cape Town, beneath the famous Table Mountain, which was either 3,000 feet high or 17,000 feet high, depending on which of two "well-informed citizens" one should believe. (The actual height is 3,549 feet.) The world tour was officially over; they sailed to Southampton, England.

For the rest of his life, Mark Twain would continue his sardonic and satirical attacks on the evils of colonialism and imperialism. in February 1901 the *North American Review* published his "To the Person Sitting in Darkness," a passionate exposé of those whom he called the "Blessings-of-Civilization Trust." Included was an account of unsavory role of Protestant and Catholic missionaries in China at the time of the Boxer Rebellion; they exacted horrendous sums from the starving population for each converted Chinese killed in battle. Another item was about Germany's role in dividing up the spoils of China: the Kaiser lost a couple of missionaries in a Shantung province riot, for which he made China pay $100,000 each, and in addition, cede 12 miles of territory worth $20 million and containing several millions of inhabitants.

Czarist Russia had entered the imperialist game by seizing Manchuria, killing countless peasants, choking its river with their swollen corpses. "Shall we go on conferring our civilization upon the people that sit in darkness, or shall we give the poor things a rest?"

That Czar Alexander II, whom Mark Twain had met on his *Quaker City* jaunt, had freed the Russian serfs; had long been eclipsed in his mind by the continued and cruel exploitation of the Russian people. On January 5, 1905, Russian troops fired on a defenseless crowd, slaughtering men, women, and children. Led by a priest, they had come to the winter palace to present a petition to Czar Nicholas II. The massacre of January 5 precipitated the abortive 1905 revolution. In March, the *North American Review* printed "The Czar's Soliloquy," by Mark Twain, in which he had Nicholas II confessing to the killings of "Bloody Sunday" with the remark, "We [the Romanoffs] have done as we pleased for centuries."

The Congo Reform Association, based in England, had been gathering horrifying stories of the atrocities committed against the Congolese people by the agents of King Leopold II, who was sole owner of the Congo Free State. They asked Mark Twain to write something about it. He responded in 1905 with "King Leopold's Soliloquy; A Defense of His Congo Rule." It was published as a pamphlet, since no publisher would touch it, was reprinted again and again and widely distributed. It played a major role in arousing public opinion and forcing the Belgian Parliament to take over the control of the Belgian Congo from their king. Mark Twain refused to take any royalties.

America did not escape the fury of his indignation for her imperialist involvements. He had, at first, approved the Spanish-American War, as a noble effort to free Cuba from Spanish domination. The subsequent American conquest of the Philippines shocked him deeply. He realized that the Filipino people were not being liberated but conquered.

Mark Twain expressed his views in "A Defense of General Funston," written in 1902, which in fact was the opposite of a defense. Funston was the American general assigned to capture Filipino President and independence leader Emilio Aguinaldo. This he had done by a trick, accepting the Filipino's hospitality, then massacring his staff. "We have robbed a trusting friend of his land and his liberty," Mark Twain commented.

He returned to American misconduct in the Philippines in an essay written in 1906, "Comments on the Killing of 600 Moros." American commander General Leonard Wood had located 600 Filipino men, women, and children, hiding in a crater on a mountain peak. His order was to kill or capture them. The Americans fired down on them "with deadly precise small arms. They left "not even a baby to cry for its dead mother."

"This is incomparably the greatest victory that was ever achieved by the Christian soldiers of the United States," was how Mark Twain summed up the shameful affair.

14

tragedy

The secret source of humor itself is not joy but sorrow.
There is no humor in heaven.

—Mark Twain

In August 1896, Mark, Livy, and Clara were living
in a house they had rented in Guildford, England,
following their world tour, and were waiting for
Susy and Jean to join them. A letter arrived from
home saying that Susy was ill. It was immediately
followed by a cablegram saying that her recovery

would be slow. Livy insisted on returning to America at once; she took Clara with her.

They were mid-ocean, when Mark received a second cablegram with the news that Susy, twenty-four years old and with the whole world ahead of her, had died of meningitis. When he could bear to write about it, he said that it was a mystery of nature that a man could receive a "thunder-stroke" like that and live. Night after night he played billiards until he dropped from exhaustion. It was the only way he could find to escape going mad with grief. Detail by detail, he pieced together what had happened.

After her parents and Clara left, Susy had stayed on at Quarry Farm, seemingly content, but during the summer of 1896 she had become restless and nervous and unlike herself. Early in 1897, she went to Hartford and stayed with Mr. and Mrs. Warner. Each day she went over to the Farmington house but found "a terrible atmosphere of lonesomeness there." She became more and more impatient for her family's return.

Kate Leary, their servant, guessed that something was wrong and made her see a doctor. He diagnosed the trouble as overwork and prescribed soothing remedies. On his recommendation she moved back to Farmington Avenue. Susan Crane and her Uncle Charlie Langdon came to stay with her and Reverend Twichell cut short a vacation in the Adirondacks to see if he could help. She became rapidly worse and her fever rose. On August 15, the doctor admitted it was meningitis. In delirium and pain she wandered through the hot empty rooms. Toward the end her sight left her. It was all over by August 18.

Her father spared himself none of this pitiful story. He even demanded the scrawls she wrote in her delirium. "To me darkness must remain from everlasting to everlasting," she had written.

That fall, Livy, Clara, and Jean went back to England to join him. They took a place in Chelsea. Mark grimly turned to writing *Following the Equator,* about the places he had visited on his world tour. He had gone back to the American Publishing Company, which since the death of Elisha Bliss was being run by his son, Frank Bliss. The Clemens family did not celebrate Thanksgiving. At Christmas, there were no presents. No one in the household felt festive. Livy's grief was as deep as Mark's; she never recovered from the blow. They had no desire to return to Hartford house and never did. Mark had often thought of it as a sentient being. "It had a heart & a soul & eyes to see us with," he once wrote Twichell. Now it was "heartbreak house."

Following the completion of *Equator,* he wrote a small book called *What Is Man?,* which had as its underlying theme the notion that man never did any deed except for a selfish motive. Livy did not care for it. He was not satisfied with it himself, and temporarily put it aside.

131

He did several stories about dreams and dream life, a subject that interested him increasingly. He had very vivid dreams himself, often dreaming the same dream over and over with variations. His most outstanding effort in this field was "Voyage in a Drop of Water," never finished. (Bernard DeVoto, who edited it for posthumous publication, and conjectured the ending from Mark's notes, called it "The Great Dark.") It is perhaps the most terrifying of all his fiction.

A man looks through a microscope at a drop of water and sees all sorts of monsters in it. The Superintendent of Dreams appears and offers to give him, his wife, and his daughters free passage on a ship which will sail through the drop of water, reducing them and the ship's officers and crew all to the proper proportions. They sail for ten years. It is always dark because the drop of water is in the shadow of the microscope. The family's own past is forgotten, but is replaced by a past in which they have always been on this ship. They grow old and gray. Storms toss them. Monster squid nearly upset them. The captain, another Ned Wakeman, utters the profanity of his profession and copes with a mutiny by admitting he has no idea where he is going and there is nothing he can do about it. Eventually the drop of water dries up and the ship is stranded on barren ground in the middle of nowhere.

The family wake up. They are back in their old home. All of two seconds have passed. They think they are in a dream and that their shipboard life was real.

It was not unusual for Mark Twain to work until four o'clock in the morning during this period in which he was writing to forget. He did his best work in bed. To Livy's embarrassment he refused to get up when reporters came to interview him. He still let her censor all his work, but certainly not to the extent some of his critics have claimed. When she objected to such words as "stench" and "offal" and "breech-clout," he commented, "You are steadily weakening the English tongue, Livy."

In December 1897, his brother Orion died in Keokuk. At the time he was simultaneously running a boarding house and writing a biography of Judas of Galilee, doomed never to be published. Mark, who had supported him for so many years, sincerely grieved for him. To Mollie, his wife, he wrote that it was unjust that such a man, against whom no offense could be charged, should have been sentenced to live for seventy-two years. Mark Twain's future writing would often express the belief that death was mankind's greatest boon. Only through death could one be free of pain and sorrow.

Financially things were coming his way again. He was staying in Vienna in January 1898, when Rogers cabled him that his creditors were paid in full and that there was money left over. *Equator* had had an advance sale of 30,000 copies. Rogers made some stock investments for him; they turned out splendidly. His fascination with inventions revived. In March he seriously considered investing in a carpet weaving machine that reproduced photographic images. Rogers convinced him not to do it.

During their stay in Vienna, he was showered with lavish hospitality. Police barriers opened up to "Herr Mark Twain." The mourning period being over; he and Livy received visitors each afternoon. Their residence became known as "a second American Embassy." It was here that Mark announced that he was a "self-appointed Ambassador at Large of the U.S. of America—without salary."

In Austria he conceived the short story "The Man that Corrupted Hadleyburg," which many critics hold is his greatest short fiction. It is a fable. Hadleyburg (still another version of Hannibal) is famed for the moral virtue of its citizens. One night a stranger leaves a bag of gold in the home of two of those upright citizens, Mr. and Mrs. Richards, with a note saying that it was to be given to an unknown person who had once done him a good deed. In time, every town notable convinces himself that he has done the good deed, or that in any case, he has the right to the gold. The stranger has managed to corrupt them all. The bag of gold brings out innate selfishness and greed, their hidden nature which has never before been revealed because temptation had never before come their way.

In October 1900, the Clemens family came back to America after their long absence. The horde of reporters who were waiting as Mark Twain walked down the gangplank of the *Minnehaha* found him hale and hearty and "as funny as ever." His triumph over debt had made him the favorite son of all middle-class America, including religious leaders and bankers. He returned to Hartford later that month but only to attend the funeral of Charles Dudley Warner. The Farmington Avenue house in Nook Farm was put up for sale.

That winter they rented a house on West Tenth Street in New York. Clara, after years of study abroad, was preparing her debut as a mezzo-soprano. They had learned several years before that Jean was subject to epilepsy. She was taking treatments from an osteopath.

In spite of his efforts to live quietly Mark Twain was hounded by interviewers who wanted his opinion on everything in the world and outside of it, including, especially, heaven and hell. His other trial was being invited to banquets given by literary and other clubs. In October 1901, he and William Dean Howells went to Yale University to receive honorary degrees. President Theodore Roosevelt was present, but disapproving. He once said that Mark Twain's criticism of missionaries made him feel like skinning him alive. The students loved him and after the ceremonies roared his name and gave the college cheer.

In late 1901 he rented a palatial mansion in Riverdale, the outskirts of New York. He was a regular guest on Henry Rogers' yacht. Andrew Carnegie, another admirer, kept him supplied with excellent whiskey. This did not prevent him from jeering at Carnegie for his self-interest and his slavish attitude toward royalty—though he did praise him for the libraries he endowed.

In May 1902, Mark Twain paid his last visit to Hannibal. During his brief stay, he let himself be photographed in front of the tiny frame house on Hill Street where he had once lived, attended Decoration Day exercises at the Presbyterian church, dined with Laura Hawkins Frazer, his childhood sweetheart who was now a widow, and at the high-school commencement exercises gave out diplomas. Before he left, photographers got him to pose again at the railroad station, holding a bunch of flowers.

The next day in St. Louis, he was welcomed aboard the *Mark Twain*, a harbor boat, and took the wheel to prove he still knew a thing or two about piloting. On June 4, the University of Missouri gave him an honorary degree in law. He quipped that if people did not call him "Doc" henceforth, "there will be a decided coolness."

He and Livy spent that summer at York Harbor, Maine, not far from the Howells' summer place at Kittery Point. Livy's health, never robust, took a turn for the worse, a combination of asthma and heart strain, the doctor conjectured. To breathe, she sat upright in her bed most of the night. A special "through train" took her back to Riverdale in October. All fall and winter, the doctor kept her in bed. When Mark could not see her, he slipped her playful and affectionate notes, sometimes in a secret code they had devised.

On the doctor's advice, he took her to Florence for the winter of 1903–1904. It was a popular notion that traveling abroad was good for one's health. They sailed in October with Clara, Jean, a nurse, Kate Leary, and Mark's secretary, Isabel Lyon. In the outskirts of Florence, he rented an enormous and gloomy villa, noticeably lacking in creature comforts. The Italian climate was as cold and disagreeable as New York's. Livy continued to grow weaker and died the evening of June 5, 1904. In his notebook, Mark wrote: "She was my life, and she is gone; she was my riches, and I am a pauper."

Jean and Clara were both ill afterwards. Clara was kept in bed until they left for New York at the end of the month.

15

a turbulent, troubled, and troublesome old age

I hear the papers say I am dying. The charge is not true.
I would not do such a thing at my age.
> —Mark Twain in a telegram to the
> Associated Press, December 23, 1909

A banquet, arranged by Harper's, his publisher, was
held at Delmonico's restaurant on December 5, 1905,
to celebrate Mark Twain's seventieth birthday. Some
200 guests came to partake of oysters, quail, green
turtle soup, red head duck, champagne, and liqueurs.
They included cherished old friends and new

acquaintances: Henry Rogers, Andrew Carnegie, Mark Twain's fellow humorists, George Washington Cable, George Ade, Finley Peter Dunne; Emily Post, Willa Cather, in fact almost everyone prominent in America's literary life. One after another they paid tribute to the guest of honor.

Much as he deplored the institution of banqueting, he gave every evidence of enjoying himself. Naturally he too had to speak. Solemnly he gave the reasons for his longevity: he never smoked more than one cigar at a time; never smoked when asleep; since he was seven he had avoided all medicine; he had never taken any exercise except sleeping and resting; he had lived a "severely moral life,"—in spite of the handicap of having been born without a single moral.

Since his return from Florence he had been living at 21 Fifth Avenue, New York. Isabel Lyon, still his secretary, had taken over the household in a manner increasingly jealous and possessive. During the period of her great influence, she convinced him that Jean belonged in a nursing home, not at home. Her reign lasted four years.

He was working on a number of projects at once, letting his imagination run riot. *A Horse's Tale* was a novelette about the love between a horse and a little Spanish girl named Cathy, much of it told from the viewpoint of the horse. The beguiling Cathy was modeled on Susy. Soldier Boy died of the vicious treatment of his captors. Cathy died trying to save

139

him. Mankind's cruelty to animals and their devotion to humans was a recurrent theme with Mark Twain.

A major project was his short novel *The Mysterious Stranger,* set in Austria in 1590, in a town called Eseldorf, an Austrian Hannibal. The young narrator, Theodore Fischer, might well be a sixteenth century Austrian Tom Sawyer.

A stranger appears to Theodore and his comrades, a handsome young man with a charming manner who wins them over, yet terrifies them. To amuse them he has a host of parlor tricks; he makes fire out of air, fills their pockets with candies, creates live animals and people out of clay—and as easily destroys them. He is an angel, he tells them; his name is Satan and he is named after his uncle. He is able to grant all their wishes but warns them they may be sorry afterwards that he has done so, for he can foretell the future and knows that disaster often accompanies those granted wishes.

When he had finished *The Mysterious Stranger,* Mark Twain put it aside. It was not published until 1916, when it was acclaimed one of the great short novels in world literature.

Another important piece written in his old age was *The War Prayer,* a powerful indictment of war. It opens in a wartime atmosphere with the "holy fire of patriotism" burning in every breast. At church on a Sunday morning, the preacher and congregation pray for God to watch over the young soldiers and help them crush the foe. A white-robed stranger enters, saying that God has sent him to grant their wish, if, after they understand what it will mean, they still desire it. He then describes the effect of their victory on the other side—the shrieks of the wounded, the destruction of their humble homes, the orphans wandering in the desolate wastes of their homeland.

It, too, was put aside to be published only after Mark Twain's death. "Only dead men can tell the truth in this world," he said. It has since been published in many editions and was especially popular with the young people who protested the war in Southeast Asia.

For years Mark Twain had fought off unauthorized biographers and unauthorized use of his letters as an invasion of his privacy. In 1906 he gave permission to Albert Bigelow Paine to do a biography of him. Once he made up his mind, he went all the way. Paine moved into a room next to his. He became his constant companion for the rest of his life and his literary executor and editor of his letters after his death.

At least since the 1870s, Mark Twain had been writing his own autobiography. On the theory that what a man thinks is more important than anything else about him, he often went off into pages and pages of digressions, so that the manuscript grew to monumental proportions. Beginning in the summer of 1906, *North American Review* printed part of it in installments. Their editor, George Harvey, called it the "greatest book of the age," as many others have done since.

With the money from the *Review*, Mark Twain bought some 250 acres near Redding, Connecticut; on the hilltop he had an Italian style villa built. Clara gave it the name of Stormfield, after a sort of fantasy he had written and which *Harper*'s magazine was publishing called "Extract from Captain Stormfield's Visit to Heaven."

This was based on a dream that Captain Ned Wakeman had once told him. At the time he had considered the subject matter too bold to publish. In the final version, Captain Stormfield traveled billions of light-years here and there after his demise and finally landed on that tiny corner of the universe reserved for earth's heaven, only to find that there were hardly any white men there at all. To every white angel, there were a hundred million copper-colored ones. And in all of heaven only a minuscule proportion could speak English.

Mark Twain, passing seventy, said that he would like very much to dress in a loose and flowing costume made all of silks and velvets "resplendent with stunning dyes." And that every man he had ever met would like to do the same but none dared. As a compromise he took to wearing snowy white suits, beginning about 1906. He took a childlike delight in the theatrical effect of his costume. The white suit won headlines in Washington where he went in December of that year to argue before a congressional committee that the copyright of a book ought to be extended to fifty years beyond the author's death. That would take care of the writer's children, he pointed out. The grandchildren could take care of themselves.

He had resolved never to go abroad again, but changed his mind when Oxford invited him to come to the university in June 1907 to receive an honorary degree. He considered this "a loftier distinction" than any other university could confer, and told Paine, his biographer, that he would be willing to journey to Mars for that degree.

His arrival in England reminded him of old times. The stevedores cheered him as he walked down the gangplank. There were more cheering and crowds lining the road as he drove to a royal garden party at Windsor Castle, where he and King Edward VII had a private chat. He lunched with George Bernard Shaw, Max Beerbohm, and Sir James Barrie. He learned a new word "Huckfinnomaniac"—a devotee of Huck Finn—applied to another writer, William Morris.

At Oxford he wore a scarlet robe and walked in a procession with the other honorary degree recipients, Rodin, the French sculptor, the French composer, Saint-Saëns, and his old and revered friend, Rudyard Kipling.

"Most amiable, charming and playful sir, you shake the sides of the whole world with your merriment," read the Oxford citation. He cherished the long red robe as long as he lived. That same year he took on the mental healer, Mary Baker Eddy, in a small book, *Christian Science,* mocking not so much the principle of mental healing, in which he believed, as Mrs. Eddy's terrible poetry and unrivaled business shrewdness.

In June 1908, he moved into Stormfield, keeping Paine with him to play billiards, which he did night after night to all hours, until Paine, the younger man, was ready to collapse. In the mornings he stayed in bed and wrote. He produced *Is Shakespeare Dead?* that year, a tongue-in-cheek support of the theory that Bacon wrote Shakespeare's plays and that, therefore, Shakespeare could not have existed as a writer.

More important was *Letters from the Earth,* purported to be letters from a Satan exiled to stay on earth, addressed to his friends, the Archangels Michael and Gabriel. In it he details what he considers the absurd notions that man has about heaven and his Creator. For instance, man, who is rarely very musical, imagines heaven as a place where he will be playing a harp all through eternity, no matter if he knows but one tune. All the things he enjoys doing on earth he leaves out of his man-made heaven. *Letters from the Earth* was Mark Twain's jolt to all the people who accept everything they are told about their religion without question, without doubt, without curiosity. Knowing it was too heretical to be published in his own time, he put it too aside, for publication after his death.

Jean joined him at Stormfield and acted as his secretary after he had explosively discharged the difficult Isabel Lyon. (In his autobiography he called Miss Lyon a liar, a thief, and a drunkard, among other epithets. There was evidence that she had mismanaged his finances to her own advantage. In the end she got her revenge, however. In 1973 a writer used her journals as the basis for a book about Mark Twain's old age. She had described him as a paranoiac and terrible old man.) After her several years in rest homes, Jean was happy to be living at home with her father again. He got acquainted with her again and found her "a surprise and a wonder."

In October 1909, Stormfield was the setting of a marriage, over which the elderly Reverend Twichell presided, between Clara and the celebrated pianist Ossip Gabrilowitsch, whom she had met in her musical studies abroad. She would be the only one of Mark Twain's three daughters to survive him. The day before Christmas that year, Jean succumbed to the last of her epilectic seizures.

Mark Twain, alone and heartbroken, remarked to Paine that he had never greatly envied anyone but the dead. One night, while playing billiards with his biographer, he had a sudden dizzy spell, the prelude to an attack of angina pectoris. He called it "tobacco heart" and tried to reduce his daily ration of cigars from forty to four, but the attacks grew more frequent and he began to lose sleep.

He sailed for a holiday in Bermuda in January 1910, but grew so weak that Paine was summoned to get him. They left for New York on April 12, with Mark Twain heavily drugged with morphine. In Stormfield, he sank into a coma from which he never awakened. He died on April 21.

That same night Halley's comet, having passed its perihelion—the point in its orbit nearest the sun—the day before, was heading toward the outer recesses of space. It was its first appearance since it had ushered in the baby Sam Clemens nearly seventy-five years before. Mark Twain had always prophesied he would go out with the comet as he had come in with it, and he was right.

mark twain's books

posthumous publications

bibliography

index

mark twain's books

THE CELEBRATED JUMPING FROG OF CALAVERAS COUNTY
AND OTHER SKETCHES
1867

THE INNOCENTS ABROAD
1869

THE GILDED AGE, WITH CHARLES DUDLEY WARNER
1873

ROUGHING IT
1872

MARK TWAIN'S SKETCHES, NEW AND OLD
1875

THE ADVENTURES OF TOM SAWYER
1876

A TRAMP ABROAD
1879

THE PRINCE AND THE PAUPER
1880

LIFE ON THE MISSISSIPPI
1883

A CONNECTICUT YANKEE IN KING ARTHUR'S COURT
1889

THE AMERICAN CLAIMANT
1892

THE TRAGEDY OF PUDD'NHEAD WILSON
1894

FOLLOWING THE EQUATOR
1897

THE PERSONAL RECOLLECTIONS OF JOAN OF ARC
1896

HOW TO TELL A STORY (sketches)
1897

THE MAN THAT CORRUPTED HADLEYBURG AND OTHER
ESSAYS
1899

WHAT IS MAN?
1906

posthumous publications

Since Mark Twain's death, a considerable amount of his writings has been published posthumously, material which he considered too controversial to publish during his lifetime, stories which he never completed, or which did not satisfy him; works originally published only in magazines or reviews. The following volumes contain some of the best of this posthumous material:

Letters from the Earth. Edited by Bernard DeVoto. New York: Harper & Row, 1962. (This volume includes *Papers of the Adam Family; Letter to the Earth; A Cat-Tale; The Great Dark*, about a voyage through a drop of water; among other shorter works.)

The Mysterious Stranger and Other Stories. New York: Harper & Row, 1950. (This volume includes *A Horse's Tale, Extract from Captain Stormfield's Visit to Heaven; A Fable*, and several shorter pieces.)

The War Prayer. New York: Harper & Row, 1968. (Illustrated with drawings by John Groth.)

There have been two versions of Mark Twain's autobiography published since his death. The first and most comprehensive was edited by his biographer, Albert Bigelow Paine. More recently an autobiography edited by Charles Neider has appeared (published by Washington Square Press as a paperback in 1961). This leaves out large sections of the Paine autobiography, includes some material never before published, and has the advantage of Mr. Neider's chronological arrangement of the material.

Between 1922 and 1925, the publisher, Harper and Brothers, published an alleged "Definitive Edition" of *The Writings of Mark Twain*, in 37 volumes. Since then, many of these volumes have gone out of print. Others, the copyright having expired, have been issued and reissued by a series of publishers. There have also been numerous collections of Mark Twain's humorous or satirical pieces, published originally in newspapers or magazines. Some of these are thought provoking. Many are hilarious. They should not be overlooked by anyone seeking relaxation or entertainment or a more complete understanding of Mark Twain's many-faceted character.

bibliography

Allen, Jerry, THE ADVENTURES OF MARK TWAIN, Little, Brown, Boston, 1954.

Andrews, Kenneth R., NOOK FARM, MARK TWAIN'S HARTFORD CIRCLE, University of Washington Press, Seattle, 1960.

Baetzhold, Howard G., MARK TWAIN & JOHN BULL: The British Connection, Indiana University Press, Bloomington, 1970.

Brooks, Van Wyck, THE ORDEAL OF MARK TWAIN, (Introduction by Malcolm Cowley), World, Cleveland, 1961.

DeVoto, Bernard, Ed., THE PORTABLE MARK TWAIN, Simon & Schuster, New York, 1946.

————MARK TWAIN'S AMERICA, Houghton, Mifflin, Boston, 1932.

Foner, Philip S., MARK TWAIN, SOCIAL CRITIC, International Publishers, New York, 1958.

Ganzel, Dewey, MARK TWAIN ABROAD: THE CRUISE OF THE QUAKER CITY, University of Chicago Press, Chicago, 1968.

Geismar, Maxwell, MARK TWAIN, AN AMERICAN PROPHET, Houghton, Mifflin, Boston, 1970.

————MARK TWAIN AND THE THREE R'S, Bobbs-Merrill, Indiana, 1973.

Hill, Hamlin, MARK TWAIN AND ELISHA BLISS, University of Missouri Press, Columbia, 1964.

Howells, William Dean, MY MARK TWAIN: Reminiscences and Criticisms, Louisiana State University Press, Baton Rouge, 1967.

Kaplan, Justin, MR. CLEMENS AND MARK TWAIN, Simon & Schuster, New York, 1966.

Meltzer, Milton, MARK TWAIN HIMSELF: In Words and Pictures, Crowell, New York, 1960.

Paine, Albert Bigelow, MARK TWAIN: A BIOGRAPHY, (3 volumes), Harper & Bros., New York, 1912.

Smith, Janet, Ed., MARK TWAIN ON THE DAMNED HUMAN RACE, Hill and Wang, New York, 1962.

Wecter, Dixon, Ed., THE LOVE LETTERS OF MARK TWAIN, Harper & Bros., New York, 1949.

————SAM CLEMENS OF HANNIBAL, Houghton, Mifflin, Boston, 1952.

index